Eating Out With
TOVEY

J O H N   T O V E Y

BBC BOOKS

OTHER BOOKS BY JOHN TOVEY

ENTERTAINING WITH TOVEY

TABLE TALK WITH TOVEY

FOOD AND FLOWERS FOR THE FOUR SEASONS
(*with Derek Bridges*)

JOHN TOVEY'S FEAST OF VEGETABLES

THE MILLER HOWE COOKBOOK

JOHN TOVEY'S COUNTRY WEEKENDS

Illustrated by Maxine Rogers
Photographs by Tim Imrie
Styling by Cathy Sinker
Edited by Susan Fleming
Food preparation for photographs and
the series by Margaret Armstrong

Published by BBC Books,
a division of BBC Enterprises Limited
Woodlands, 80 Wood Lane, London W12 0TT

First published 1988

© John Tovey 1988

ISBN 0 563 21431 7 (Hardback)
0 563 21430 9 (Paperback)

Set in 11 on 13pt Bembo, and printed and bound in
Great Britain by Butler & Tanner Ltd, Frome and London
Colour printed by Chorley & Pickersgill Ltd, Leeds
Jacket/cover by Fletchers of Norwich

Eating Out With
TOVEY

CONTENTS

ACKNOWLEDGEMENTS

I'd like to thank my loyal, devoted long-standing staff, without whom this book and the TV series would have been impossible.

INTRODUCTION

———··———

Each winter I travel abroad with six of my staff for two to five weeks with the assistance of British Airways, dispelling the myth that English food consists of overcooked tough beef and soggy cabbage. It is a marathon tour, and involves hugely detailed advance organisation. It also demands a degree of charm and skill, as we discovered when we had to face customs officers in Tokyo the day after Paul McCartney had been found with cannabis. The airport was seething with armed police set to uncover any grains of illegal cargo, and I was rather nervous as one of our five trunks contained two large sacks of Lakeland hay (in which to bake leg of lamb)!

The over-excited officials stared with disbelief, and smiled a little at the first opened trunk holding, as it did, saucepans, ladles, knives, chopping boards, saws, knife sharpeners etc; at the sight of the second trunk containing kitchen whites, uniforms, teatowels, J-cloths and muslin, they giggled; the third, which contained food processors and mixers, they thought too much so they didn't bother to open the other two. I literally aged meanwhile as, had they opened the trunk containing the hay, all hell would have broken loose!

We open our 'festival', as it is called, in a chosen hotel in the chosen city, and quickly settle in after the invariable hiccups of the opening day, evolving a daily pattern which will cause as little inconvenience as possible to the hotel's own chefs. We spend all day cooking for the dinner at which anything from 50 to 500 guests will be present. Each evening the restaurant is 'dressed', a pianist or harpist plays sentimental English pieces such as 'I left my heart in an English garden' or 'A nightingale sang in Berkeley Square', and the overture is always, but always, 'Greensleeves'. Guests are escorted to their tables, lights dimmed and the performance begins.

When it's all nearly finished, as the coffee is being served, the chefs and I rush to our rooms, shower and change into very smart, navy blue Miller Howe emblazoned blazers and slacks, and appear to take our bows as ambassadors of English cooking. My speech always starts off with 'Let me tell you that Great Britain is still *great* and, provided you start your holiday by flying our national carrier, British Airways, you will find a warm welcome, extremely good food and lodgings from John o'Groats to Land's End, and fine value. However, the English Lakes must be your main objective, situated as it is in the greatest National Park in the country. It is called the "Gateway to Heaven".' People usually sit up at this stage and I have a captive audience. (On one occasion recently in New York, though, a lady guest exclaimed in the loudest stage whisper during my theatrically planned pause, 'Yes, Scotland is marvellous, isn't it?' Much mirth ensued, but I got my own back – and even more laughter – when I uttered one word in a similar stage whisper, articulating just what I thought of her.)

And of course the Lake District *is* marvellous. Quite apart from its magnificent scenery and its wealth of cultural and literary associations, it has also become virtually world-famous for its food. Well-hung Lakeland lamb is hard to better; freshly caught char from the bed of Lake Windermere now find plenty of takers locally (they were once, in the age of the stagecoach, potted and sent down to fashionable London gentlemen's residences). Our Cumberland hams (how I hate, loathe and detest the modern word Cumbria, and I always head my notepaper 'English Lakes'), cured by Mr Woodall of Wabberthwaite, soon disappear from butchers' racks, and I hesitate to imagine how many tons of Cumberland sausages are loaded into visitors' cars to be taken home. The northern shore of Morecambe Bay sports the famous shrimps and fluke fish. Damsons abound in the Lythe Valley and the 'cheese' made from them goes so well with mutton. Weekly markets still sport stalls of other traditional home-made produce – jams, butters, cheeses, chutneys, preserves, pickles and bakes.

As far as ingredients are concerned, the Lake District is abundantly supplied. Equally so, of course, we are rich in restaurants, hotels, boarding houses and cafés, many of which are deservedly listed and lauded for their cooking in the endless guidebooks and food guides. I often find it hard to credit the number of really good eating places there are in so small, relatively speaking, an area. Admittedly it is an area to which people flock each year, but sometimes tourism works *against* quality. Not so here.

So, to share with you both the beauties of the area, and to give you a more literal 'taste' of the Lake District, we have selected some sites and landmarks, showing a cross-section of our heritage, which is to be hoped will long remain enticing visitors to our Park annually. However, at the end of the day, even though you may be enraptured at the scenic beauty amidst which my colleagues and I are fortunate enough to have to work, those of us associated with making the series this book accompanies are anxious to motivate you in another way.

We would like you immediately to want to rise from your chair, switch off the telly, get into your kitchen and commence cooking! Good food produces good friends, and for me the greatest joy in life is to have people round my table 'breaking bread and supping wine,' in its turn, surely the oldest pastime in life.

As the programmes continue you will, I hope, find several dishes that instantly appeal to you. There could be some you turn your nose up at – shame – but *all* are served at some time or another at Miller Howe (we'd soon be out of business if we didn't deliver the goods to our clients). Every single dish is within your capacity and skill, and every recipe has been double tested. The ingredients should be easily obtainable from your local suppliers, and none of the recipes is terribly time-consuming or expensive (I'm presuming you *will* push the boat out just a little for special guests). Most can be prepared and served to your guests with apparent ease. What you have to remember, though, is that any recipe is 'difficult' to prepare the first time – you'll be feeling your way, with a degree of doubt and uncertainty – and you'll take slightly longer than you will the second time. Always, but always, try a new recipe out on the family, not on treasured guests!

I have a good life in the Lakes, if a hard-working one, and there are many perks. One of them is working for *Lloyd's Log* as their food correspondent. This takes me to various parts of the world meeting interesting people, sampling some wonderful food, and – more import-ant still – titillating my mind and palate with new ideas and com-binations of flavours. In fact, I definitely do think that travelling – foodwise – has helped me to maintain and improve my standards of cooking.

It does have its bad points, too, though. Take my tour of Australia, where I was faced with 43 meals in 26 days from Brisbane across country to Perth. Not happy with this, my editor called me in Sydney suggesting I stop off in Bombay en route home and stay at the Taj Mahal to eat in all their restaurants and sample room service. Getting home, I felt like the original Michelin man. As I eased my blubber out of the sud-filled bath, I took a frank look at my sagging, portly self and said aloud, 'You are disgusting'. A friendly voice from the open-plan lounge said, 'Think positively'. I took another look and did just that, saying, 'You are positively disgusting'!

But when I come home to the Lakes and fall back into my self-imposed routine of walking from home to the hotel, and being dragged by Ossie, my Old English sheepdog, across the fells, the spreading bulge is kept at bay. However much I love travelling – and I literally thrive on it – I always look forward to returning to that part of England that has been my home for so long – to the stark beauty of the distant Langdale Pikes, the peace of the lake at night, the fresh winds blowing across the fells, and the wonderful and salutary open-air, often damp, walks, surrounded by bleating sheep. As a food lover and unrepentant meat eater, I hope I may be forgiven for tending to appreciate these typical Cumberland animals rather more for their potential as a roast in hay . . .

I hope that in our television programmes and in this book, we have succeeded in giving you a true 'taste' of the Lake District, an appreciation of the beauties which surround me daily and which are so accessible to all of you. I hope too that in the recipes included here, and those ideas elaborated in the series, I have been able to communicate and inspire you with my ideas on 'eating out'.

CHAPTER ONE

BREAKFASTS & BRUNCHES

So many people skimp on this meal these days in the false hope that by so doing they can burn off any fat or alcohol accumulated from the day or night before. Not so. It's not good for you, nor is it very productive, to start the day empty: the old wives' tale of 'go to work on a full stomach and you'll have a full day' is much more accurate.

A good breakfast needn't be cooked: you could have some grapefruit or other citrus segments – lots of Vitamin C to keep colds at bay – or some grated apple and carrot in yoghurt. A large bowl of home-made muesli – anything and everything you can find in the local health food shop, mixed together – served with milk or yoghurt, can provide energy, fibre, protein and lots more besides. These only take minutes to prepare, but many of my cooked breakfast suggestions can be served up pretty quickly if you spend a little time and effort on them the night before. My porridge, for instance, can be cooked and served in less than 20 minutes if you've soaked the oats overnight in milk to soften and enrich them. The Lakeland platter, too, can be made up ready on its trays the night before, and then it will be ready in 30 minutes from start to finish. Similarly with the popover batter, and the fish custard dishes.

All this pre-preparation can mean that you have time for a walk before breakfast – a healthy necessity for me with an Old English sheepdog to exercise – and come back with an even more healthy appetite. For those who might have to work before breakfast – like Mr Douglas Freeman of Town End Farm, Troutbeck – it's doubly important to have something substantial and nourishing to come home to. He looks after a flock of Swaledales and a few Rough Fell sheep, and although it's a healthy life, and the fells are beautiful, I don't envy him the all-weather nature of his work. (His daughter is also a shepherdess, apparently, and often works on horseback!)

For an ideal balanced breakfast, I would recommend a fruity starter – perhaps just a glass of freshly squeezed orange juice, although *my* favourite is orange juice with sparkling wine, Buck's Fizz – followed by something cooked from the following pages. Even something simple like a chunk of Cumberland sausage served with some delicious home-made chutney can be considered. Thereafter you could toast slices of the no-need-to-knead nutty wholemeal bread on p. 84, and spread with one of the marmalades or lime curd.

As well as preparing in advance, good shopping is of the essence when relatively simple fare is being cooked for breakfast. It goes without saying that fresh free-range farm eggs should be used; they *can* still be found, and the flavour is well worth the effort. Bacon, too, should be 'real' – none of those vacuum-packed slices which sizzle away to nothing in the pan. Always buy bacon with the rind on – this, when cut off, can help start off many frying processes, and not just for breakfast.

GRAPEFRUIT SEGMENTS *10*

BAKED SMOKED HADDOCK SAVOURY *17*

LIME CURD POPOVERS *23*

——— · • · ———

OVERNIGHT PORRIDGE *13*

BAKED LAKELAND PLATTER *14*

——— · • · ———

GRAPEFRUIT SEGMENTS

——— ·•· ———

Grapefruit segments make a delicious starter for breakfast, and many people believe that the acids in this fruit help break down any fats lingering from the night before, and that your body is thus cleaned out first thing in the day. Grapefruit are so much better these days than they were in my childhood, as they have been developed to give a juicier fruit with less and less pith.

We all must, at some time or another, have suffered the indignity of being presented with half a fresh grapefruit in some hotel dining room: it will have been cut in half by the breakfast chef using the same knife he used for rinding the bacon and cutting open the kidneys, and then he will have made a bungling attempt to separate some of the segments. Not only is the taste tainted, but the struggle to get the juicy bits from the pith and skin uses up so much energy, one is exhausted before the day even begins!

To counteract this, I serve fresh grapefruit already segmented, *out* of its skin. I use one whole fruit per person which might sound extravagant, but when segmented, they don't look so much. Served this way they can be eaten with a teaspoon easily and effortlessly; they can also look stunning if served in a crystal saucer champagne glass on a doyleyed plate with a fern and small flower from your garden border. For further splendour, you could dip the edges of the glasses before filling in egg white and some sugar coloured with green colouring or cochineal.

For an extra touch you could add a generous dribble of crème de menthe (gets the bloodstream working again after a sluggish night before) or scatter with toasted sesame seeds (p. 11) – or you could do a *medley* of segments – grapefruit, orange and lime perhaps – with sprigs of fresh mint. Another addition might be thickish slices of peeled, cored apple, which will eke out this breakfast starter dish, and add lots of goodness.

To prepare grapefruit segments (and any other citrus fruits), you need a very sharp, preferably serrated, knife, and a sieve placed over a bowl (the sieve to catch the segments, and the bowl the juice). Lay the grapefruit down on the work surface, stalk end to one side, and lop off a slice from each of the two ends left and right. Turn the grapefruit over to stand on one of these flat ends, and you should see all the exposed top flesh with the membranes separating the segments spanning out from the middle looking a little like bicycle-wheel spokes. The next thing to do is to remove all the skin and white pith. Hold the grapefruit in your non-working hand with thumb on one exposed end and fingers firmly supporting the opposite exposed end. Sawing backwards and forwards with the sharp knife, remove a strip of skin about 1 in (2.5 cm) wide which, if cleverly and carefully done, curving round the shape of the fruit, will simply do this and not hack away any of the juicy flesh. Having taken one section off, it is relatively simple to go round the fruit, removing all the skin and pith in the same way. Occasionally one does leave behind some pith so before going on to the next stage, simply nick this all off with your knife.

Hold the completely peeled grapefruit in the palm of your non-working hand with the white lines of the segments' membranes running across the palm of your hand. Slowly 'saw' the knife down each side of these white skin lines – on each side of the actual segment – and, if done gently enough, the knife's movement will halt as it hits the centre core. The segments, one by one, are gently separated from the membrane and core, tipped into the sieve, and the juices allowed to run through into the bowl underneath. Squeeze the debris to get out all the juice. It may sound tricky but it is well worth the trouble.

SESAME SEEDS

Toasting sesame seeds gives them a nuttier, more interesting flavour as well as texture, and they can be used in a variety of ways as you'll see throughout this book.

To toast, simply spread them out on a baking tray and put them into an oven you have pre-heated to about gas mark 4, 350°F (180°C) (preferably for something else, not just the seeds). Keep on taking the tray out and turning the seeds with a wooden spoon until they are nice and golden brown. Bring the outside edges into the middle each time – the edges brown first. A tray holding 4 oz (100 g) seeds browns nicely in 20–30 minutes. Store in an airtight tin.

GRATED APPLE AND CARROT WITH YOGHURT

——— · • · ———

The textures are interesting, and help to make this fine healthy dish. Prepare it just before serving – it doesn't take long.

· serves 2 ·

10 oz (275 g) natural yoghurt
1 large apple
2 smallish young carrots
a little freshly grated nutmeg or ground cinnamon
(optional)
toasted chopped nuts (optional)

Whisk the yoghurt and put it into a large bowl. Simply wipe the skin of the apple with a damp cloth, and then, using a stainless steel grater, coarsely grate it (avoiding the core, of course) into the yoghurt. Using young carrots (better as they will be sweeter), top, tail and peel them (put the peelings, if they are not too dirty, into the stock pot if you have one on the go), and then grate into the yoghurt as well. Mix the ingredients together, and divide between two serving dishes.

A little grated nutmeg or cinnamon will add further flavour. And for health-conscious folk, toasted walnuts, pecans, pistachios or hazelnuts – sesame seeds, even – can be scattered on top of this dish just before serving (*not* beforehand, as the nuts will go a trifle soggy). To toast nuts, simply do as for the sesame seeds in the previous recipe.

OVERNIGHT PORRIDGE

This is very yummy and could be a treat when out walking on the fells provided you have a wide-lipped thermos flask similar to those used for soups. In fact, as it only takes 20 minutes to heat through and finish off, it should be on your agenda for most cold wintery days. For everyday breakfasts, a drop of the cream from the top of the milk is all that is needed, but for those special occasions when entertaining at a weekend, I like to dish the porridge out into the warmed dishes and then put the merest coating of malt whisky over the surface with a generous blob of farm butter and a good sprinkling of either soft brown or demerara sugar. A sprinkling of wheatgerm is also healthy and you could put yoghurt on top and dribble runny honey over for sweetening!

· per person ·

2 oz (50 g) porridge oats
10 fl oz (300 ml) milk

The night before, put the oats into a Pyrex or china bowl and cover with the milk. Cover with foil and leave in a warm place overnight; this can be the airing cupboard, on top of your central heating boiler or – as at Miller Howe – in an oven with only the pilot light burning.

Next morning stir together and place the bowl over a pan of boiling water. Heat gently, stirring occasionally, and in 20 minutes the porridge is ready to serve.

BAKED LAKELAND PLATTER

———— · • · ————

Guests at Miller Howe will have tried this from the breakfast menu –
and indeed I've outlined the principles before. It's such a doddle,
though, as long as you've shopped sensibly and prepared the night
before, that I can't resist giving the recipe again. All the organisation
can be done then, and the trays will be put in the pre-heated oven on
the following morning in the order indicated. I can't think of anything
more guaranteed to delight and fill weekend guests.

· per person ·

butter
$1\frac{1}{2}$ in (4 cm) chunk of Cumberland sausage
1 rasher good smoked or green back bacon
1 slice apple
lemon juice
2 mushroom caps (save the stalks for use in something else)
$\frac{1}{2}$ tomato
salt, sugar and freshly ground black pepper
a few slices of par-boiled peeled potato
1 triangle crustless bread
1 egg

Butter the baking trays very well. Prick the sausage, rind the
bacon, brush the apple slices with lemon juice and top the mushrooms
with tiny knobs of butter. Brush the tomato halves with melted butter
and season with salt, sugar and pepper. Leave on a baking tray or trays
in the fridge. All this, even the par-boiling of the potatoes, can be done
the night before.

When you wish to cook, pre-heat the oven to gas mark 4, 350°F
(180°C), and allow 30 minutes' baking altogether. Arrange the sausage
on a baking tray and put in the pre-heated oven. Add the bacon to this
tray after 15 minutes. Dip the bread triangles in melted butter and
arrange with the apple, mushrooms and tomatoes on another tray.
These go into the oven for 10 minutes, 5 minutes after the bacon.

Meanwhile, you can be frying the potato slices in butter. At the
very last moment you can cook the eggs: it's easy to fry for·up to four
guests; more, and I suggest you serve scrambled.

Serve on hot plates, and revel in the compliments!

KIDNEYS WITH SHERRY

——— · • · ———

· *serves 6* ·

1 lb (450 g) lamb's kidneys, halved, cleaned and skinned
2 oz (50 g) butter
6 oz (175 g) onions, peeled and finely chopped
5 fl oz (150 ml) cooking sherry

Cut the kidneys into manageable, edible pieces, removing and discarding any tough cores. Melt the butter in a pan, and fry the onions until golden. Add the prepared kidneys and cook for 2 minutes only, making sure they are sealed on all sides. Bring the heat up to its absolute maximum and pour on the sherry. Shake the saucepan vigorously, and continue to cook for *1 minute only*. Serve at once with heart-shaped or round croûtons (p. 127), or the following French toast soldiers.

FRENCH TOAST SOLDIERS

——— · • · ———

These are also very good served with the smoked haddock savoury on p. 17.

· *makes 16 soldiers* ·

butter
4 bread slices, crusts removed
2 eggs, beaten
2 tablespoons milk
salt and freshly ground black pepper

Pre-heat the oven to gas mark 6, 400°F (200°C), and lightly butter a baking tray.

Cut the bread slices into 4 fingers each. Mix the beaten eggs, milk and seasonings and dip the soldiers well in this. Lay on the greased baking tray and bake in the pre-heated oven for 10 minutes. Turn them over and continue baking for 10 more minutes.

SALMON CUSTARDS IN SMOKED SALMON

This is a devilishly indulgent dish, basically a quiche without the fattening pastry. Serve for a posh breakfast, or as the starter at a supper party.

· *serves 6* ·

butter
6 thin slices smoked salmon, each large enough to wrap
round the inside wall of a ramekin
12 oz (350 g) fresh salmon, skinned and diced
15 fl oz (450 ml) double cream
3 eggs plus 2 egg yolks
salt and freshly ground black pepper

Pre-heat the oven to gas mark 5, 375°F (190°C), and butter 6 × 3 in (7.5 cm) ramekins well. Line the 'walls' of the ramekins with the slices of smoked salmon. Divide the fresh salmon cubes between the ramekins.

Beat the cream with the eggs, egg yolks and seasoning, and pour over the salmon in the ramekins.

Put all the ramekins into a bain-marie – a roasting tin with $\frac{1}{2}$ in (1 cm) boiling water – and bake in the pre-heated oven for approximately 30 minutes until set. Serve on small doyleyed plates with a teaspoon.

Serve different ingredients in the same proportions in the cream custard for easy variations: prawns with a mere touch of Pernod; smoked haddock flakes with some grated cheese on top of the custards prior to baking; or chopped smoked bacon with finely chopped leeks.

BAKED SMOKED HADDOCK SAVOURY

This little fishy savoury is one of the recipes which can be basically prepared the night before, and then baked through in the morning.

· *serves 6* ·

1 lb (450 g) smoked haddock on the bone
1 pint (600 ml) milk
1 bay leaf
6 black peppercorns
2 oz (50 g) butter
2 oz (50 g) plain flour
1 fennel bulb, finely chopped
5 fl oz (150 ml) double cream
2 oz (50 g) fine breadcrumbs
2 oz (50 g) Cheddar cheese, grated

for the garnish
sprigs of fresh dill or parsley

Pre-heat the oven to gas mark 4, 350°F (180°C), and lightly butter and season 6 small heatproof serving dishes.

Poach the smoked haddock in a pan with the milk, bay leaf and black peppercorns for 5 minutes. Remove from the heat and allow to cool. Drain the haddock well and flake the flesh from the bones and skin. Discard the latter and put the flesh to one side. Strain the milk and keep.

Melt the butter in a pan and add the flour to make a roux. Cook this for about 4 minutes over a medium heat, and then little by little beat in the flavoured milk until you have a thick sauce. Fold in the chopped fennel, double cream and then the flaked haddock.

Divide this mixture between the serving dishes and when you wish to serve put the dishes in a bain-marie and heat through in the pre-heated oven for 15 minutes. Remove, sprinkle with the mixed breadcrumbs and cheese, and finish off under a very hot grill. Serve garnished with sprigs of dill or parsley.

HOME-MADE LIME CURD

·•·

A delicious variant on my lemon curd and it's just as useful: serve on toast at breakfast, use in the popovers following, on tea breads or scones at tea, or in flans.

· *makes about 10 oz (275 g)* ·

4 oz (100 g) unsalted butter
8 oz (225 g) caster sugar
juice and finely grated rind of 3 limes
4 egg yolks

Place the butter, sugar, lime rind and juice together in a bowl over a pan of simmering water. Heat to melt and beat together with a wooden spoon until quite smooth.

Drop in the egg yolks, beat in well, and continue cooking until the mixture will coat the back of the wooden spoon – run your finger along the coated back of the spoon and if the line remains quite clearly, the curd is ready. Never *overcook*, as the curd will set and thicken further while it is cooling. And never let the water in the pan boil too fiercely, or the yolks will *cook*. In all, it should take about 45 minutes.

Pour the curd into warmed clean jam jars or pots. Eat within a couple of weeks.

Opposite: A selection of spreads for a sunny breakfast (see pp. 18 and 24–7). At the back, from the left, home-made lime curd and three-fruit marmalade. At the front, Seville orange marmalade and tangerine and apricot spread.

Overleaf: For a picnic lunch on the fells, you could start off with some carrot and parsnip soup kept hot in a thermos (p. 69), accompanied by slices of nutty wholemeal bread (p. 84). Follow with a foil-wrapped chicken breast stuffed with banana and mango, baked in smoked bacon (p. 76), or some puff pastry rounds (p. 72). For those with a sweet tooth, carefully pack a duotone blender cheesecake – here made with coffee and rum and strawberry (p. 80).

LIME CURD POPOVERS

The basic batter for these popovers – little, sweet Yorkshire puds and a delicious finale to a breakfast – can be made the night before which saves a little time. You can replace the lime curd with jam or marmalade.

· makes 8 popovers ·

olive oil
4 oz (100 g) plain flour
a pinch each of salt and freshly grated nutmeg
2 eggs
5 fl oz (150 ml) cold milk
3 tablespoons single cream
8 teaspoons lime curd (p. 18)
icing sugar

Pre-heat the oven to gas mark 7, 425°F (220°C), and put a little oil into 8 holes of a muffin or popover tin.

Sieve the flour, salt and nutmeg into a bowl and make a well in the centre. Beat the eggs, milk and cream together and pour into the well. Start to mix, gradually drawing in the flour from the edges, until you have a smooth, bubbling batter. Cover with a teatowel and leave for an hour or so (or overnight in a cool place).

When you want to cook, remove the teatowel and beat 1 tablespoon of oil into the batter. Put the oiled tin into the oven to heat through thoroughly, then remove and pour enough batter into each hole to come two-thirds up the sides. Spoon the teaspoon of lime curd into the centre of each popover and place immediately in the hot oven. Bake for 25 minutes, when they should be very crisp and puffy. Sprinkle with icing sugar and serve hot.

Opposite: A substantial breakfast could start off with some grated apple and carrot with yoghurt (topped with toasted nuts if you like), and continue with a hearty baked Lakeland platter, including sausage, bacon, mushroom, tomato and apple (pp. 12 and 14).

THREE-FRUIT MARMALADE

——— · · ———

Using three fruits gives a wonderfully rich flavour to this marmalade, but you could, of course, ring the changes by using only grapefruits, oranges or lemons, or half and half orange and grapefruit, or two-thirds lemons to one-third limes. The *method* is the same, but the flavour can be infinitely varied once you have mastered the basics.

· *makes about 10 lb (4.5 kg)* ·

$1\frac{1}{4}$ lb (500 g) each of Seville oranges, grapefruits and lemons, well wiped
6 pints (3.3 litres) water
6 lb (2.7 kg) sugar

Wash your preserving pan (or your largest aluminium saucepan) really well: sprinkle it with salt and then scrub with a lemon half before rinsing with cold water and drying. Cut the fruits in half, and squeeze out the juice on a juicer, then pass through a nylon sieve into the cleaned dried pan. Have ready a 15 in (38 cm) square of clean muslin and into this scrape out the juiced flesh and pith of each of the fruit; add the pips and shreds of flesh from the juicer and sieve. Tie up securely. Cut the fruit skin into very fine strips using a sharp knife, and add to the pan of juice along with the measured water. Suspend the tied-up muslin bag in the pan – hang it from a wooden spoon balanced across the pan.

Simmer the water, juice, rind and the muslin-contained flesh and pips for about 2 hours, or until the mixture is reduced by half. (Mark the original level on the outside of the pan with a pen or pencil, and this will make it easier to calculate.) Remove from the heat. Hold a strong sieve over the pan and remove the soggy muslin bag to this. Press down hard with a wooden spoon so that as much juice as possible is extracted from the pulp and pips. Discard the dry contents of the muslin. Meanwhile, warm the sugar in a low oven. (Ideally this should be preserving sugar, but granulated works too.)

Replace the pan over a gentle heat and begin to add the warmed sugar, 1 lb (450 g) at a time, never adding the next lot until the first has melted. Stir well with each addition. When all the sugar has been added and has melted, bring the mixture to the boil and, stirring from time to time, boil until the setting point is reached, about 15–20 minutes.

To test for setting, if you have a sugar thermometer, half immerse it in the bubbling liquid. If it registers 220–222°F (104–105°C), the marmalade should be ready. If you don't own a thermometer, don't panic. Place 3 saucers in the freezer and, when you think setting point has been reached, place about a dessertspoon of the liquid in one of the cold saucers. Leave for a second or two and if it crinkles when pushed with your finger and feels tacky, it's ready. If it's still runny, return to the heat and continue boiling; test again with one of the remaining cold saucers. Meanwhile, warm some clean, dry jam jars in a low oven.

When ready, remove the pan from the heat and skim off any scum from the top. As the marmalade cools, spoon it into the jars to within an inch or so of the top. Cover with a waxed disc and then, after wiping the jar clean, with a cellophane circle held in place with an elastic band. Leave to cool completely and store in a cool dark place.

SEVILLE ORANGE MARMALADE

—— ·•· ——

A Mrs Keiller of Dundee used to make quince or *marmelo* preserve until one day her husband bought up a job lot of an unknown fruit, the Seville orange. Being a good Scot, rather than letting them go to waste, she made a preserve from them and thus marmalade – and indeed a famous marmalade company – was born.

· *makes about 10 lb (4.5 kg)* ·

3 lb (1.4 kg) fresh Seville oranges, washed
2 lemons, washed
6 pints (3.3 litres) water
6 lb (2.7 kg) sugar

Cut all the fruit in half and squeeze out the juice and pips into a sieve over a large bowl; also spoon out as much pith and juiceless flesh as possible into muslin as in the previous recipe. Add the pips and any pulp to the muslin and tie the bag up securely. Slice the fruit skins finely and add to the bowl with the juice. Add the water and immerse the bag in the juice and water mixture overnight.

Wash your preserving pan really well as in the previous recipe. Put the juice, rind and water mixture into the pan and suspend the bag from a wooden spoon in the liquid. Bring to the boil and simmer as in the previous recipe, for about 2 hours, until the volume has reduced by half.

As in the previous recipe, remove the muslin bag and squeeze, add the sugar, boil to setting point, test, and then pot.

TANGERINE AND APRICOT SPREAD

The tangerine segments in this spread 'explode' when bitten into, and the whole thing is delicious on hot buttered toast. If tangerines are not available, use an appropriate amount of clementines instead.

· makes about 6–8 lb (2.75–3.6 kg) ·

12 tangerines
8 oz (225 g) dried apricots, soaked in 5 fl oz (150 ml)
cooking brandy overnight
juice and rind (cut in julienne strips) of 2 lemons
$1\frac{1}{2}$ pints (900 ml) water
$1\frac{1}{2}$ lb (675 g) demerara sugar

Cut 6 of the tangerines (skin as well) into quarters, remove pips, then blend coarsely in your food processor. Remove the peel from the remaining 6 tangerines and carefully cut this into very thin strips. Remove any pith and pips from the tangerine segments. Cut the apricots up finely – into roughly 12 bits each.

Put the blended tangerines with the lemon and tangerine rind strips, lemon juice and water into a large saucepan. Bring to the boil and then simmer until reduced by half, about 2–3 hours.

Remove from the heat and fold in the sugar. Return to the heat and bring back to the boil. Fold in the chopped apricots and tangerine segments, bring back to a rolling boil, and continue to cook for 5–10 minutes, stirring occasionally with a wooden spoon.

Test for setting as on p. 25 and if it's ready, allow to cool slightly before potting.

CHAPTER TWO

LUNCHEONS

For a lunch (or indeed dinner) that is slightly more formal, perhaps for larger numbers, pre-planning is vital so that everything goes smoothly. Although balancing hot dishes against cold is a prerequisite of every menu (we all have limited oven and warming space), it's particularly important with larger numbers. If you have to go above the basic recipe quantities in this book – usually for six or eight – then I would advise you to try and have a different temperature dish either side of the main course to simplify things: cold dishes before and after a hot main course, for instance. Most of the cold dishes can be prepared at least a day in advance, which further simplifies matters!

As my favourite types of lunches are those in summer when we can eat outside, I have chosen basically summery foods – salmon, salads, chicken, peaches etc. I don't think you'll find anything too difficult here, and all are easily amplified to feed more.

And what more splendid place to hold a sophisticated summer luncheon than at Holker Hall, known quite justifiably as 'Cumbria's premier stately home'. Its history goes back to the sixteenth century, and it has been owned and lived in by only three families since then – the Prestons, Lowthers and Cavendishes. The Cavendish family took possession of Holker in 1756, and there are still Cavendishes living in Holker now. It is a large and very pretty house – a deeply loved family home – set amidst beautiful gardens not far from Morecambe Bay. It is open to the public and has items of interest other than the house itself – the Lakeland Motor Museum and a Craft and Countryside Museum among them, for instance.

M E N U   O N E

PARSNIP, CUCUMBER AND RED PEPPER SALAD *52*

BAKED SALMON STEAKS *43*
WITH BLENDER HOLLANDAISE *159*

FRESH PEACH CREAM PIE *61*

———— · · ————

M E N U   T W O

MARINATED SEAFOOD SALAD *46*

ROAST BARBECUE-COATED CHICKEN *49*

ROULADE *58*

———— · · ————

CURRIED HERBED WHEATMEAL PASTRY

————·•·————

Margaret Costa started her brilliant *Sunday Times* article in May 1974 about my pastry by saying that wives, mothers and lovers so often feel a sense of inferiority when they are unable to make, cook and serve delicious pastry. Well, I reckon your love life will definitely improve after you have successfully tackled any of the pastries in this book!

It was this article that gave Miller Howe its initial build-up of publicity in the USA and was the reason for an invitation from the veteran food writer, Craig Claiborne of the *New York Times*, who wanted to witness me make this pastry and two others. I will never forget the experience.

We had to collect Mr Claiborne from his flat near the Carnegie Hall and take him to his house in the Hamptons by chauffeur-driven limousine as he had just, the night before, returned from a four-week visit to the West Coast. It was a dark, cold, bleak, windy dawn with heavy snow showers forecast later on in the day. This added to my panic as I had to catch the last flight from New York to Washington where the whole pastry procedure was to be repeated for the *Washington Post*! I had taken my own ingredients over from the UK along with balls of pastry frozen and packed in containers. It was a nightmare up in my suite at the Pierre Hotel attempting to make sure the butter was soft, some balls of pastry pliable, and others chilled so that all would go smoothly.

The limo collected me and I was introduced to the great man himself on the sidewalk. He seemed ill-tempered as apparently his flight had been 3 hours late the night before and he had had a lot of trouble with the central heating in his city apartment. The silence of the journey to the Hamptons was broken only by grunts and groans as he opened his backlog of mail.

Eventually I was settled into his kitchen and he, sitting on a high stool with photographer and assistants in the background, told me to start. I weighed out a pound of flour and as I was passing it through a sieve on to the work surface, was acidly asked, 'Just what are you doing?' It was surely perfectly obvious to even the most unenlightened what I was doing, and why the great man had to make an issue out of it beat me ... until it dawned on me, quite quickly ... I was beginning to work with a weighed pound of flour, whereas Americans, of course, work with virtually nothing but cups.... Never to this day will I understand why I was so stupid. I stuttered and stumbled, fumbled and nearly freaked out and finally got myself into such a state of nerves I simply stopped. A glass of wine was suggested – and offered – and all I can now say is that many bottles of wine later I just managed to catch my flight to Washington and Mr Claiborne eulogised my pastry in his paper!

It goes without saying that the main thing needed for light pastry is a light hand and a light heart! The first time you make this one I am sure you will be pleased (if you follow the instructions carefully, of course), but my, oh my, by the third time the ease with which you make it and its superb texture will make you glow with pride – and indeed, might improve your love life!

This pastry can make bases for sweet tarts or flans too. Omit the parsley, curry powder and salt, and use 3 tablespoons icing sugar instead.

· *makes 3 × 10 in (25 cm) quiche or flan bases* ·

8 oz (225g) wheatmeal flour
8 oz (225 g) plain flour, sieved
2 level tablespoons finely chopped parsley
1 level tablespoon curry powder
a pinch of salt
10 oz (275 g) soft butter
2 eggs plus 1 egg yolk

Mix the flours together well with the parsley, curry powder and salt, and place on the work surface. Make a well in the centre and into this place the butter. Pat down on it to make firm indentations and then break the eggs on to the butter with the extra yolk. Carry on patting and dabbing for about 8 minutes until you get a scrambled eggs texture.

Lift up the flour from all four edges using a palette knife and put on top of the butter-egg mixture. Now start cutting through the mixture with the same palette knife. Do so quickly, and at an angle of 90 degrees, scraping along the bottom of the work surface occasionally so that the butter is evenly distributed throughout the flour.

When the mixture begins to look like a shortbread mixture, stop. Divide it into three parts, and form each very gently into a rough ball. Do *not* squeeze. Put the balls into individual bags and leave to chill – or indeed freeze.

To bake, allow the pastry to come back to the texture it had before chilling. To make a quiche base, lay the base of a 10 in (25 cm) loose-bottomed flan tin on the work surface and flour around its edges. Place a ball of pastry on the base and persuade it out gently with your hand. Roll until it overlaps the base edges by enough to make the sides of the flan. Fold these overlaps back over the base and insert the base into its ring. Push the overlaps back into shape around the sides and use any pastry excess to make 'sausages' to reinforce the edges of the base. Chill for at least 30 minutes.

To bake blind, pre-heat the oven to gas mark 3, 325°F (160°C) and line the pastry case with foil and baking beans, taking particular care to cover the rims. Bake for 30 minutes, then turn off the oven and remove the foil and beans. Keep in the oven for another 5–10 minutes if you think the flan case isn't cooked enough – too pale on the base or too soft.

To make savoury tartlets with this pastry, do exactly as above, but obviously on a smaller scale. Cut into 3 in (7.5 cm) rounds, and bake blind for 15–20 minutes only.

CURRIED WHEATMEAL PASTRY QUICHE

Serve the quiche while still slightly warm as a lunch or dinner starter, cut into 8 wedges. Garnish with a little savoury salad (p. 132). A more substantial slice of quiche could be wrapped in cling film and taken on a picnic.

· serves 8 ·

1 × 10 in (25 cm) blind-baked wheatmeal pastry flan case
(p. 33)
filling of choice (see below)

for the custard
10 fl oz (300 ml) double cream
2 eggs plus 1 egg yolk
salt and freshly ground black pepper

Pre-heat the oven to gas mark 5, 375°F (190°C), and place the blind-baked flan case ready on a baking tray.

To make the custard, simply mix all the ingredients together. Place the additional filling ingredients in the base of the flan case, and pour in two-thirds of the custard. Put in the pre-heated oven and bake for about 10 minutes. Pull the oven shelf out a little way and spoon in the remainder of the custard. This prevents custard being spilled when taking the quiche to the oven, and also ensures that the quiche will puff above the rims. Leave to bake on for about another 25 minutes, until firm and golden, then remove from the oven.

QUICHE FILLINGS

CHICKEN, BACON AND RED PEPPER

6 oz (175 g) cooked chicken, chopped
4 oz (100 g) cooked smoked bacon, finely diced
2 oz (50 g) red pepper, cleaned and finely diced

CHICKEN LIVER AND WATERCHESTNUT

8 oz (225 g) chicken livers, cubed and marinated in 2
tablespoons sweet sherry for at least 4 hours
4 oz (100 g) waterchestnuts, chopped

SALAMI, ANCHOVY AND OLIVE

8 oz (225 g) good salami, skinned and cubed
6 anchovy fillets, soaked in 2 tablespoons milk for a couple
of hours
12 stoned black olives

SUN-DRIED TOMATO

A new firm favourite of mine is this quiche made with bottled sun-dried tomatoes which come in a delicious herbed olive oil (*never* throw this away, but use in one of the blender dressings on p. 55). Unfortunately, I find if I open a jar, they all disappear before I have a chance to use them, as they're a devilishly moreish commodity. They're also delicious with French sticks: split the French sticks open, dribble the oil from the tomatoes on top, with the tomatoes, and heat through in a very hot oven... However, for the quiche, add to the custard 10 oz (275 g) drained sun-dried tomatoes. It's even nicer if you add, with the second lot of custard, 2 oz (50 g) well toasted pine kernels.

CHEESE AND HERB PÂTÉ

I don't know what I'd do without this basic, it appears in so many of my recipes. It can be used in a multitude of ways, among them as the base of savoury salads, between the skin and flesh of a chicken to be roasted, as a lining for a savoury gâteau, as the filling for a canapé tartlet or a stuffed fresh date canapé, and as a garnish for many foods, including plain cooked veg. Store in the fridge.

· makes 1 lb 6 oz (625 g) ·

5 oz (150 g) butter
1 lb (450 g) good cream cheese
3 garlic cloves, peeled and crushed with a little salt
1 tablespoon each of finely chopped chervil, parsley and
chives (or any fresh herbs available)

Melt the butter very slowly in a small pan. Using an electric hand-beater, mix the other ingredients together in a large bowl, making sure the herbs are evenly distributed.

When the butter has cooled a little, pour it slowly and carefully into the cream cheese mixture. Fold in carefully, as it could curdle. When all has been absorbed, spoon the pâté into a bowl or loaf tin, and leave to cool thoroughly and set.

Opposite: This magnificent new lunch or dinner starter dish (p. 140) consists of an avocado mousse set on a curried digestive biscuit base, with cheese and herb pâté up the sides. It is topped with concasse tomatoes and toasted sesame seeds.

Overleaf: For a sunny lunch in the garden, serve a plate of marinated seafood salad (p. 46) or a slice of a quiche – here made with sun-dried tomatoes and pine kernels – as a starter (p. 37), followed by barbecued individual portions of marinated chicken (p. 49).

BAKED SALMON STEAKS

When you buy salmon at your fishmonger it is invariably sold in steaks with the messy bones in the middle and scaly skin on the outside. I have to agree with food pundits who say steaks cooked like this with the bone in the middle gain from the flavour and juices in the bones. However, salmon steaks prepared in the following manner are so easy to cook and serve, and, more important still, simple to eat! Particularly so if you are having to entertain large numbers.

First of all you take a whole salmon of about 8 lb (3.6 kg), and remove the head and tail. Gut it in the usual way through the belly, but then lay the fish on its side and, starting at the tail end, cut half-way through the fish right along the backbone. It might sound tricky, but if you have a sharp serrated knife, you can do this with ease. Remove the long backbone, and then lay each separated side skin down on your work surface. Using the same knife and in a sawing action, at a 45 degree angle to the skin bring the flesh away from the skin. You now literally have what appears to be two sides of salmon similar to that when smoked, but minus the skin!

It is now a relatively simple task to portion these sides into the size of steak *you* wish to serve. When you wish to cook, pre-heat the oven to gas mark 8, 450°F (230°C). Generously butter a baking tray and put 1 oz (25 g) salted butter on each steak. For steaks of about 6 oz (175g), bake in the pre-heated oven for 6 minutes, and serve with blender hollandaise (p. 159) and some delicious vegetables. Or you can serve the steaks cold; see a few ideas on p. 93.

Opposite: For a substantial starter, or a light lunch or high tea dish, serve a half avocado stuffed with cheese and herb pâté and baked in bacon (p. 94). Garnish with a croûton topped with chutney and a twirl of cheese and herb pâté (p. 38). This also makes a good pre-dinner canapé.

POTTED SPICED SALMON

——— ·•· ———

I adapted this recipe from a seventeenth-century cookbook – *The Accomplisht Cook* by Robert May – for the tercentenary issue of *Lloyd's Log*. It makes a delicious and unusual starter.

· *serves 6–8* ·

$1\frac{1}{2}$ lb (675 g) boned and skinned salmon, finely cubed
10 fl oz (300 ml) double cream
juice of $\frac{1}{2}$ lemon

for the marinade
10 fl oz (300 ml) dry white wine
2 teaspoons white wine vinegar
6 sprigs fresh dill
1 sprig each of fresh thyme and marjoram
1 bay leaf
2 sage leaves
a pinch each of ground ginger and freshly ground nutmeg
2 teaspoons runny honey
2 tablespoons demerara sugar
$\frac{1}{2}$ teaspoon black peppercorns, crushed
finely grated rind of 1 lemon
2 cloves

for the garnish
fresh dill

Place the salmon cubes in a large heatproof bowl. Place all the marinade ingredients into a pan, bring to the boil, and pour over the salmon. Mix well and, when cold, cover with cling film and leave in the fridge for 24 hours. Mix the cream with the lemon juice, cover and leave that in the fridge as well for 24 hours. The cream will sour and thicken.

The next day, strain the salmon, discarding the marinade, and pat dry on kitchen paper. Fold carefully into the soured cream and divide between 6–8 × 3 in (7.5 cm) ramekins. Cover and leave to rest in the fridge before serving. Garnish with fresh dill and offer fingers of buttered brown bread.

GRAVADLAX

—— · • · ——

A wonderful new version of marinated salmon – it melts in your mouth! Serve as the Scandinavians do, by itself or on buttered bread for an open sandwich, or in the trio of salmon dish on p. 142 or the marinated seafood salad following. See p. 43 for how to prepare a salmon, and then cut one of these boned sides in half.

· *serves 2* ·

½ side skinned and boned fresh salmon (p. 43)
½ bottle rosé wine
finely grated rind of 2 oranges
1 teaspoon finely grated fresh ginger
walnut oil
4 tablespoons coriander seeds
1 tablespoon black peppercorns
4 oz (100 g) fresh dill
6 tablespoons coarse sea salt
16 tablespoons demerara sugar

Cut the piece of salmon through horizontally, and place in a dish. Mix the rosé wine with the grated orange rind and finely grated fresh ginger, pour over the salmon, cover and leave for 24 hours in the fridge.

Remove the salmon from the marinade and dry the pieces on all sides. Paint all sides with walnut oil.

In a liquidiser mix the coriander seeds, black peppercorns and fresh dill. Remove this mixture from the liquidiser and stir together with the coarse sea salt and demerara sugar.

Cut a piece of foil large enough to enclose the fish completely. Lay it flat on your work surface, dull side upwards, and put a third of the coriander mixture in the middle. Spread it out so that when you place one of the oiled pieces of salmon on it, the fish is fully covered. Put another third of the mixture on top of this, and place the other piece of salmon on top. Finish off with the balance of the coriander mix. Bring up the sides of the foil and seal tightly. Leave in the fridge for at least 3 days.

MARINATED SEAFOOD SALAD

——— · • · ———

Without any doubt this is my favourite new dish this year, and when served at Miller Howe always elicits favourable comments from delighted diners. After you have read the recipe you may well say to yourself that all this faff is not for you. But believe you me, as all the preparation is done the day before, it leaves you with only the assembly of the actual dish prior to your guests' arrival. There is wonder and excitement as each leaf is removed and yet another kind of fish is revealed, and it's a masterpiece of varied textures and flavours.

· serves 6 ·

a variety of salad leaves – use Webbs, endive/frisée, chicory,
iceberg, radiccio, oakleaf etc
at least 3 blender dressings (p. 55)
6 oz (175 g) smoked salmon, cut into 1 oz (25 g) slices
6 oz (175 g) *gravadlax* (p. 45), cut into 1 oz (25 g) slices

for the scallops
6 scallops, cleaned
a little natural yoghurt
juice and finely grated rind of 1 lime

for the langoustines
6 langoustines, (or scampi 'tails')
1–2 oz (25–50 g) garlic butter (p. 153)
a little blender mayonnaise (p. 57)
toasted desiccated coconut

for the sole
2 fresh lemon sole fillets, skinned
1 bay leaf
a little grated fresh ginger
3 fl oz (75 ml) dry white wine
4 black peppercorns

for the fresh salmon
6 oz (175 g) fresh salmon, cut into 6 thin circles
5 fl oz (150 ml) dry white wine

Prepare the scallops, langoustines, sole and fresh salmon first, to allow them time to cool.

For the scallops, put them in a small pan with the yoghurt, lime juice and rind, bring to the boil and simmer for 3 minutes. Turn out immediately into a cold dish.

The meat of langoustines – miniature lobsters – is in the abdomen and tail. Shell as you would a prawn or shrimp, removing the black spine thread. Reserve the shells and claws. (Or use fresh or frozen scampi 'tails'.) Fry the prepared langoustines in the garlic butter to seal them, then turn the heat off and stir from time to time until they are cold. *Just before serving*, coat them with the mayonnaise and dip into the toasted desiccated coconut.

Cut the flesh of the sole into finger-sized strips and place in a shallow heatproof dish. Place the skin, bones and the langoustine shells and claws (if available) in a pan with the bay leaf, ginger, wine and the peppercorns, and bring to the boil. Pour through a sieve on to the sole strips, and leave to cool. When cold cover with cling film.

Place the fresh salmon in a shallow heatproof dish, and pour the boiling white wine over. Leave to cool, then cover with cling film.

When you wish to serve the salad, prepare 6 individual salad bowls or plates. Divide the leaves into 6 portions, and paint each with one of the dressings – the individual flavours of different dressings adds interest to the finished salad. Have ready all your slices and strips of fish, drained if necessary, including the smoked salmon and *gravadlax*. On each plate build up a circle of the dressed salad leaves with a different fish portion cleverly hidden in between.

SOLE AND SALMON EN PAPILLOTE

There is nothing new about cooking inside greaseproof paper – but so few people actually do it! It is essential that you obtain very good quality greaseproof paper, otherwise with the wine and butter your parcels could well disintegrate in cooking. *Never* use foil as a substitute, even though it has a stronger texture and is a better conductor of heat. It's just not the same.

· *serves 6* ·

butter
salt and freshly ground black pepper
6 oz (175 g) boned and skinned salmon
6 oz (175 g) boned and skinned sole
18 very small mangetouts, washed
1 large carrot, peeled
dry white or rosé wine
freshly chopped fresh herbs (optional)

Pre-heat the oven to gas mark 4, 350°F (180°C), and butter six square pieces of greaseproof paper well. Season the buttered paper with salt and pepper.

Cut the salmon and sole fillets into chip-sized pieces. Top and tail the mangetouts, and remove the back veins. Cut the carrot into 1 in. (2.5 cm) lengths with a very sharp knife, and then cut each length into very thin strips. Blanch these strips in boiling water for no more than 10 seconds just to take the hard crunch out of them!

Divide all the ingredients between the six buttered and seasoned sheets of greaseproof paper, and then sprinkle the wine over them, as if you were putting vinegar on your fish at the fish and chip shop. (It's even nicer to add some chopped herbs at this stage.) Push the ingredients to one triangle side of the square, and season. Lift the uncovered triangle of paper and fold over the top. Make a double fold round the two open sides, and make a twist at the three tips for a secure parcel.

Place on a baking tray, and bake in the pre-heated oven for 12 minutes. Take to the table in the paper, and allow guests to open their own parcels, thereby enjoying the wonderful smell as well as taste.

Roast Barbecue-coated Chicken

Occasionally people have gasped when they first see this dish on their plates as, when cooked, it looks rather burned – but of course it isn't.

· serves 6 adequately and 4 generously ·

1 × 3 lb (1.4 kg) fresh chicken
6 oz (175 g) soft cheese and herb pâté (p. 00)

for the marinade
3 tablespoons olive oil
1 tablespoon walnut oil
2 tablespoons tomato paste
1 dessertspoon Worcestershire sauce
freshly ground black pepper
$\frac{1}{4}$ teaspoon sea salt, crushed
1 dessertspoon soy sauce

Dry the fresh chicken well and place in a dish. Pull back the skin at the neck to expose the breast flesh. Work your hand in carefully to fully separate breast and legs from the skin. Using your hand, stuff the cheese and herb pâté between the skin and flesh of the breasts and drumsticks.

Paint the chicken all over with the mixed marinade and leave in the fridge in a dish fully covered with cling film. Over the period of 2 days, whenever you go into the fridge, from time to time lift the cling film and paint more of the marinade on.

When you wish to cook, pre-heat the oven to gas mark 4, 350°F (180°C), and roast the chicken for $1\frac{1}{2}$ hours, basting every 15 minutes with the marinade. This slightly longer cooking time, plus the cheese and herb pâté, makes the skin succulent, and the flesh juicy and well cooked.

To barbecue the chicken instead of roast it, stuff with cheese and herb pâté, marinate and chill well. Quarter the bird, and wrap each portion tightly in foil, with 1 tablespoon of the barbecue marinade in each parcel. Over hot barbecue coals, the breast portions will take 20 minutes, the legs 30–40 minutes. There's no need to turn them.

CHICKEN, PEACH AND BACON SALAD WITH MINT JULEP DRESSING

——·•·——

One of my favourite dishes for an informal light lunch, even better on a warm sunny day. It is an idea I got in New Orleans where I fell for the mint juleps I imbibed while listening to the local jazz.

· *serves 6* ·

2 × 3 lb (1.4 kg) fresh chickens, cooked exactly as in the
recipe on p. 49
6 smoked bacon rashers, rinded
salad leaves, as varied as possible: Webbs, Cos, oakleaf, curly
endive etc
at least 5 fl oz (150 ml) mint julep dressing (p. 55)
3 fresh ripe peaches

for the garnish
watercress sprigs

Prepare and cook the chickens exactly as in the recipe on p. 49. As the chickens are cooling, cover them with cling film and make sure the lovely juices are *not* thrown away as these will set to a very sloppy jelly to be used in the dressing. You only need the 4 breasts for this recipe, so you can use the remainder of the chickens in another recipe.

Cut the bacon into very small pieces with scissors and fry gently in a small frying pan until very crisp indeed. Drain off the fat, retaining it for future use, and leave the bacon bits on one side to cool.

Using a very sharp, serrated carving knife, slice the breasts of chicken very thinly and put on a serving platter. If you go into the meat with an away-from-you action, you will be pleased with the number of thin slices you get from each side of the breast.

Arrange as many varied lettuce leaves as you can on individual serving plates, setting them out as prettily as possible. Mix a little of the dressing with the jellied juices from the chicken, and sprinkle over the leaves on each plate, followed by the cooked bacon dice.

Halve the peaches and cut each half into very thin wedges. (Some people insist on peeling peaches, but personally I prefer the slightly tough texture rather than wasting flesh when taking off the skin.) Arrange chicken slices alternately with peach slices on top of the salads on the plates. Pour the balance of the dressing over the dishes just as you take them to the table (it could be served slightly warm). I like to garnish this dish with tiny end sprigs of watercress.

Variations could include croûtons in the salad base and a few segments of orange.

PARSNIP, CUCUMBER AND RED PEPPER SALAD

——— · • · ———

I still firmly believe that parsnips taste much better after they've had a frost on them – it does for them what sunshine does for garden peas! However, this may just be me, as they seem to be available most of the year and are always tasty. (Like me, do you resort to cutting them into chip-sized portions and popping them round the Sunday joint for its last 30–40 minutes' cooking? They're so absorbent, they literally take up the fat and are so wicked, but oh so nice!)

The rough texture of the grated parsnip in a salad as here, goes well with the limpish, but positive, taste of the cucumber, and the sweet and juicy red peppers are such a good complement. You can serve the salad with soured cream as here, or with some herb mayonnaise (p. 56).

· *serves 6* ·

10 fl oz (300 ml) double cream
juice of $\frac{1}{2}$ lemon
at least 12 lettuce leaves, wiped
some blender dressing of choice (p. 55)
$\frac{1}{4}$ cucumber, wiped and scored (p. 130)
1 whole red pepper, wiped, seeded and cut into very small
pieces
2 large parsnips, peeled and coarsely grated

for the garnish
sprigs of fresh herbs

First of all, mix the cream with the lemon juice to sour it, and leave in the fridge – this sometimes takes up to 3 hours.

Dress the lettuce leaves with the dressing, and arrange on individual plates. Cut the scored cucumber into very thin slices and divide these between the 6 plates, arranging them in a circle on top of the lettuce.

Mix the chopped red pepper and the grated parsnips into the soured cream and then portion on top of the cucumber circle. Garnish with sprigs of fresh herbs. Tarragon is particularly good, but a sprig of parsley will set it off nicely.

Parsley, Rice, Egg and Red Pepper Salad with Walnuts

—— · • · ——

There are two varieties of parsley, the curly and the flat or Continental. I think parsley must be the best known and most widely used herb as it grows in profusion in herb gardens, along borders or in little pots and tubs; it has a delicate, distinct and piquant flavour, and is full of iron and Vitamin C. My grandmother used to make parsley tea and sweeten it with parsley honey which she made each autumn.

If you have a surfeit of either parsley, use it in this most unusual and titillating salad – much more interesting than just as a garnish – and although you might be horrified at the vast amount of parsley needed, believe me it goes nowhere. . . . The breaking off of the parsley heads from the stalks (which can be bitter) is very time-consuming, but draw a stool up to your work-top, and have some decent music on in the background.

· *serves 6* ·

8 oz (225 g) long-grain rice
10 fl oz (300 ml) home-made chicken stock (p. 67)
4 eggs, hard-boiled
walnut oil
1 garlic clove, peeled and halved
5 fl oz (150 ml) walnut and smoked bacon dressing (p. 55)
4 oz (100 g) parsley heads, weighed after stalks are removed
1 red pepper, wiped, seeded and finely chopped
24 walnut halves, roughly chopped
soured cream (optional)

Put the rice and chicken stock into a pan and bring to the boil. Turn the heat down and simmer until the stock has been absorbed and the rice is *al dente*, about 15 minutes. Leave to cool.

Cut the eggs in half and separate the yolks and whites. Pass both through separate sieves. The yolks are easy, but you may have to resort to a sharp knife and chopping board for the whites!

Brush a serving bowl or bowls liberally with walnut oil and then press the garlic pieces all over the surface. Pour in the walnut and bacon dressing and place the parsley heads, rice, peppers and walnuts on top. Toss to mix, then decorate with the egg yolks and whites. A dessert-spoon of soured cream on top of each portion is delicious.

BLENDER DRESSINGS

I can remember in the early sixties when I first came into the hotel business, the actual making of French dressing for use in the dining room was done with style and flair by the *maître d'* and the junior *commis* chef always had to have to hand a tray full of the necessary ingredients for this task: a small birch whisk, gleaming silver-plated teaspoons and a tablespoon, an old-fashioned china soup bowl, all covered with an immaculate, stiffly starched, plain white teatowel. Nowadays the two most important things to me are a blender and my own tasting finger!

I love making French dressings, as they are never the same twice running, particularly these days as I like to thin them down with the dregs of wines from opened bottles, and experiment with the many oils available. There again, on the spur of the moment, I will take out a screw-top jar and shake up a dressing simply by opening the store cupboard at the farm and use, occasionally, quite bizarre ingredients such as soy sauce, liquid from a piccalilli jar, lemon curd, redcurrant jelly.... Even just reading this may make your toes curl, but once you take the plunge and experiment, you will be pleased with your confident culinary skills!

First of all I give you the basic requirements, with some additions for variations. These are all rather gutsy dressings, particularly if you use a good strong olive oil, but for health freaks or those particularly conscious about diets, every one of them can be made with a lighter oil and can be thinned down using 10 fl oz (300 ml) white or rosé wine. The dressing doesn't cling as lovingly to the salad, but at least the flavours are slightly diluted!

· *makes a good pint (600 ml)* ·

1 pint (600 ml) oil of choice
3 tablespoons white wine vinegar
a generous pinch of English mustard powder
1 teaspoon caster sugar
a pinch each of cayenne pepper and salt

To make the *basic* dressing, simply whizz the oil, vinegar and seasonings in your liquidiser. While it's whizzing, if you like, add the extra ingredients as below.

VARIATIONS

—— · • · ——

ORANGE AND HONEY

Add the juice and grated rind of 2 oranges, and 2 tablespoons
runny honey.

CORIANDER AND NUTMEG

Add 1 level tablespoon whole coriander seeds and a $\frac{1}{2}$ nutmeg,
freshly grated.

WALNUT AND SMOKED BACON

Add 5 fl oz (150 ml) each of walnut oil and the fat from cooked
smoked bacon.

MINT JULEP

Add 2 egg yolks, 5 fl oz (150 ml) bourbon, the juice of 1 grapefruit
and 12 leaves of fresh mint. This dressing is best if a *light* oil, like
grapeseed, is used.

WATERCRESS AND ORANGE

Add the juice and grated rind of 2 oranges, and the leaves only from
a small bunch of watercress (this might require a little extra sugar).

TURMERIC AND LEMON

Add 1 tablespoon turmeric and the juice and grated rind
of 1 lemon.

MAYONNAISE

This is the original mayonnaise, and although it might take longer to make than the following blender mayonnaise, it is beautifully creamy and delicious, and I think there is no real comparison in flavour.

· makes 10 fl oz (300 ml) ·

2 egg yolks
a few drops of lemon juice
$\frac{1}{2}$ teaspoon each of dry English mustard powder,
salt and caster sugar
10 fl oz (300 ml) good olive oil
1 tablespoon white wine vinegar

Place a bowl on a damp teatowel or cloth on the work surface so that it will remain stable during the beating. Put in the egg yolks, lemon juice, mustard, salt and sugar, and beat together with an electric hand whisk. Measure the oil into a jug and, dipping the fingers of your free hand into the oil (the other hand is holding the whisk), dribble these drops into the bowl, the whisk whizzing away at top speed. When these dribbles have been absorbed, continue thus until you've blended in about two-thirds of the oil.

It will be fairly thick. Add the vinegar and mix in, then pour in the balance of the oil in a steady trickle, still beating away at top speed.

You can adjust the basic flavour of the mayonnaise by adding more or less mustard or sugar, or by using different vinegars (but *never* malt), or even oils. Vary your mayonnaise more drastically as below. Store in a jar in the fridge.

HERB

Add 2 tablespoons of a single finely chopped herb or mixed herbs.

AVOCADO

Add the mashed flesh of a very ripe avocado.

CITRUS

Add the juice and finely grated rind of 1–2 lemons or oranges.

TOMATO

Add 1 tablespoon tomato purée or paste.

CURRY

Add curry powder to taste.

GARLIC (AÏOLI)

Add 3 crushed garlic cloves.

BLENDER MAYONNAISE

The original mayonnaise above is definitely superior, but this blender version is excellent for speed, and for when you want to prepare large quantities. It's ideal, too, for the fish recipe on p. 147. It isn't quite as smooth and rich as a conventional mayonnaise because of the presence of the egg whites.

Both mayonnaises can be used in a variety of ways. Obviously they are delicious with cold chicken breast or cold salmon steaks, and they can be used as a base for flaked salmon or prawns and put in a tartlet case. But think too of serving them with avocados, with a pear or a cored apple as a savoury starter. The latter will be even more tasty if, for 6, you blend 2 oz (50 g) each of banana, walnut and stoned fresh dates, and use this as a base for the mayonnaised apple.

· *makes 10 fl oz (300 ml)* ·

3 eggs
10 fl oz (300 ml) good olive oil
1 tablespoon white wine vinegar
2 teaspoons caster sugar
1 teaspoon made English mustard
$\frac{1}{2}$ teaspoon salt

Put the eggs in the goblet of your blender or processor, and while it is running, dribble in the olive oil. When that has all been absorbed, put the machine on top speed. Mix the remaining ingredients together and drop in and mix well.

As with a conventional mayonnaise, you can add a variety of ingredients to flavour the basic mix (see previous recipe).

CHOCOLATE AND RUM ROULADE

—— · • · ——

Roulades – those colourful cartwheel cakes, made without flour – make many people nervous, but there really is no need as they are relatively easy to prepare and cook – and they're a delight to serve and eat. As with so many of my recipes, once you've mastered the basic principles, you can go on to invent all sorts of variations for yourself. I'll take you carefully through the stages of the basic recipe for one version, and beneath indicate how you can make some alternatives.

· *serves 6–8* ·

melted butter
6 eggs, separated
6 oz (175 g) caster sugar
6 oz (175 g) good plain chocolate, broken into pieces
2 tablespoons dark rum

for the filling
15 fl oz (450 ml) double cream
3 tablespoons caster sugar
3 tablespoons dark rum

Stage 1. Beforehand

The first thing you'll need is a shallow-sided tin measuring about 11 × 14 in (28 × 35 cm), and this needs to be lined with proper silicone paper. Staple the corners to make a paper container to size within the tin. Grease this well with melted butter.

Pre-heat the oven to gas mark 4, 350°F (180°C), and try to double-check the temperature if you can. Even the slightest variation in temperature can be disastrous when baking roulades. Use an oven thermometer if you have one.

If you have a copper bowl – cleaned with a cut half lemon and some salt – it's ideal for beating up the egg whites to exactly the right consistency.

Stage 2. Preparing the Roulade Mixture

Put the egg yolks in a warmed bowl and beat them to a ribbon – for at least 5 minutes – until white and light. Then, little by little, beat in the sugar. The whole process should take at least 12 minutes.

In a double saucepan, for this particular roulade, melt the chocolate pieces with the rum. Leave to cool fractionally.

Meanwhile begin to beat up the egg whites, in the copper bowl if you have one. You want them to be stiff.

Transfer the egg yolk and sugar mixture to a large plastic bowl and pour the melted cooled chocolate in through a sieve. Fold in well. (For the other roulades below, fold in the dry flavouring ingredients at this stage.) Fold in one-third of the stiffly beaten egg whites, then beat the remainder of the egg whites back to a stiff consistency (they can flop quite quickly). Fold these in, using a long-handled metal spoon.

Turn the mixture out into the buttered paper-lined tray and spread evenly across – don't *push* – and into the corners.

Stage 3. Baking the Roulade

Place the filled tray in the carefully pre-heated oven and bake for 20–30 minutes. To ensure that it's ready, bring the tray gently half-way out of the oven and insert a thin skewer in the middle. If the roulade is cooked, the skewer should come out completely dry. The top should be crisp and cracky too.

Take the roulade out of the oven when it is ready, and cover the top with a clean, dry teatowel. Cover this in turn with a well dampened teatowel, and you'll see the steam rise. This settles the crisp top, and will make the roulade easier to roll when it's cool. Leave to cool in the tin, preferably overnight.

Stage 4. Turning Out

Cover a wooden board larger than the roulade tin with foil and then a double thickness of good greaseproof paper. Put this board, papered side towards the roulade, on top of the roulade tin, and invert the tin on to the board. The roulade will come out, its paper casing on the top.

You need now to remove this paper casing, but don't do it in one fell swoop, as you might tear bits of the cake away. Lay one hand on the paper towards one end of the roulade, and tear the paper off in *strips*. It takes longer, but better to be safe than sorry.

Stage 5. Filling and Rolling

You can really use anything you fancy to fill a roulade, but the simplest, often the most delicious, filling is whipped flavoured cream. Whip the cream up with the sugar and alcohol, and then spread over the whole roulade surface.

To roll, start at the long end nearest you and, lifting the ends of the double sheets of greaseproof paper and foil the roulade is resting on, give the roulade a little push away from you. Carry on pushing, and it should roll well.

Stage 6. To Finish

Cut off about 1 in (2.5 cm) at each end of the roulade to neaten, and then carefully lift – you'll need two fish slices or an extra pair of hands – on to a pretty serving platter. Sprinkle with icing sugar for that final touch.

ROULADE VARIATIONS

CHOCOLATE AND BRANDY

Simply replace the rum in the basic recipe with brandy.
This roulade is rather good at Christmas.

COFFEE AND HAZELNUT

Instead of the chocolate and rum, fold into the beaten egg yolks 4 oz (100 g) ground hazelnuts mixed with 2 level tablespoons powdered Nescafé coffee.

MANGO AND COCONUT

Instead of the chocolate and rum, fold into the beaten egg yolks 4 oz (100 g) toasted desiccated coconut with 1 fresh mango, peeled and then the flesh coarsely grated.

FRESH PEACH CREAM PIE

———— ·•· ————

· serves 6–8 ·

1 × 8 in (20 cm) sweet wheatmeal pastry flan case,
blind-baked (p. 33)

for the filling
5 egg yolks
3 oz (75 g) caster sugar
juice and finely grated rind of 1 lemon
10 fl oz (300 ml) double cream
1 lb (450 g) fresh ripe peaches, stoned and segmented

for the topping
3 egg whites
6 oz (175 g) caster sugar

Pre-heat the oven to gas mark $\frac{1}{2}$, 250°F (120°C), and put the flan
case ready on a baking tray.

For the filling, put 3 of the egg yolks plus the 3 oz (75 g) sugar
and lemon rind and juice into a glass bowl and place over a pan of
simmering water. Cook for about 15 minutes, stirring occasionally
with a wooden spoon, until the mixture begins to thicken. Remove
the bowl from the pan and leave to cool.

Beat the cream lightly with the remaining 2 egg yolks and then
fold into the cooled custard filling. Spread this mixture over the base
of the flan case and arrange the segmented fresh peaches on top, in rings
if you like, or all over, pressing them into the custard.

For the topping, whip up the egg whites, adding the 6 oz (175 g)
caster sugar little by little until of a meringue texture, thick and grainy.
Pipe this over the top of the pie, and put into the pre-heated oven.
Cook for 1 hour. Leave to go cold, for at least 6 hours, so that the
custard base has a chance to settle and firm.

CHAPTER THREE

PICNIC LUNCHES

Picnics can be either a pain or a joy. If you do intend to go for a proper picnic, put your whole heart and soul into the adventurous spirit of the occasion, and don't be penny-pinching. Take the best and serve the best, and make a real production number of it. Many foods can be more easily transported than you might think, especially if you travel by car, have loads of rigid containers and baskets and boxes to hold them, and a number of willing hands.

The bubbly paper used for wrapping expensive china comes in very handy for wrapping picnic china and dishes, for it's always better, I think, to have proper plates rather than paper. Large cardboard boxes are good too for holding everything; those used for wine bottles should be kept intact with the bottle dividers, for packing the actual glasses you are going to use for the wine. The only plastic items could be the inexpensive sets of disposable Italian plastic cutlery (the makers may think it's disposable, but I've had some now for several years which I have religiously transported home, washed, dried and stored away!). They are firm to the hand and sharp to the cutting.

Other picnic pampering might include a car rug or two. Years ago these were actually used in cars devoid of heating, and often old-fashioned, stone hot-water bottles were taken along for the ride to keep the joints from freezing up completely. (I even remember windscreen wipers having to be wound up: and on one occasion on the East Coast, these had to be literally flipped from left to right from the inside by hand when the clockwork mechanism seemed to freeze up in the intense cold.)

Large umbrellas can come in useful for the odd spot of rain, but even in Britain they could hold off strong sun! I often take one firm freezer box filled with boiling water and washing-up liquid for washing one's hands with J-cloths – they dry easily enough in the open air. And don't forget to take an insecticide spray as on one occasion we were besieged by the most minute pestering midges which seemed to get everywhere.

That's how I would *ideally* picnic, but even a picnic 'on the hoof', so to speak, such as Marjorie enjoyed on the fells with Mr John Wyatt, can be substantial and delicious: a thermos of hot soup can warm, and a foil-wrapped chicken breast, veal roll, or a puff pastry round can fill! Mr Wyatt was particularly interesting as he has recently retired as a National Parks Warden, and indeed has been commissioned to write a history of the National Parks. There are ten of these in the country, and Mr Wyatt was the second warden to be appointed for this area. Wardens' responsibilities include the safety of walkers and climbers (they're quite often called upon to rescue people from the fells and hills, using specially trained dogs), and the maintenance of the parks – badly worn paths, damaged fences etc. For all this, the preservation of my beloved Lake District, they have to rely greatly on voluntary helpers.

Basic Cream of Vegetable Soups

There is no doubt at all that soups are simple to make, but simply super! They can be served in smaller bowlfuls as the first course of a lunch or dinner; as a soup course, as at Miller Howe; or in larger bowls or mugs as a major part of a casual or picnic meal. They're easy to prepare, and once you have grasped the basic method, you can ring the changes almost indefinitely – by altering the basic vegetable ingredients, by altering the *proportions* of those ingredients, or by garnishing the soup in a different way. I think my soup recipe is one of the most useful and delicious in my whole culinary repertoire – I hope you do too!

Frozen prepared vegetables can, of course, be used, but for the pocket and the palate, *fresh* is still the best. However, you can seek out bargains at your local greengrocer for soups: cauliflowers which aren't as white as you would select for a straight vegetable, will make excellent soup, and you can enhance/change the flavour by using cheese, caraway seeds or herbs; root vegetables are invariably an inexpensive buy throughout the year, and by experimenting with herbs and spices you will be amazed at what excitement you can create.

A criticism sometimes passed about my soups is that they are too thick. Should this be your opinion, simply add further stock or milk to achieve the consistency *you* desire. This can also mean that you can serve *more* people with the soup. I usually reckon on my thick recipe serving 12 small bowlfuls, or 6 larger ones. Dilute further, and you can stretch the soup even more. Don't go *too* mad though.

And a good stock is vital for the best flavour. For a basic poultry stock – fish or vegetable stocks can be used, too, as appropriate – gather together poultry bones, skin and trimmings (cooked or uncooked) and put them in a large pan with vegetable flavourings. These can be anything (except potato), but try always to have some onion, carrot and celery. Don't turn your nose up at vegetable trimmings: the ends and papery skins of peeled garlic, the discarded skins and green bits of tomatoes, the clean peelings of carrots etc. Fill the pot with cold water and toss in a few parsley stalks, a couple of bay leaves and a handful of black peppercorns. Bring to the boil, then turn down and simmer for at least 4 hours. It's really too easy for a specific recipe, but basically you're trying to *extract* flavour from the ingredients into the water, so simmer slowly, and add anything else that you think might *contribute* to the flavour of the water and the ultimate stock.

My soups are always seasoned just prior to eventual serving. Salt, pepper and sugar immediately come to mind, for not even the greatest cook can *guarantee* an eventual superb flavour: it is common sense to realise that basic vegetables will vary according to the time of the year, and to how Mother Nature has treated them.

With my North Country background, my freezer is never without a choice of at least three different soups, and when I make a soup I always prepare sufficient to put some away for future use. Soups are best frozen in ice-cube trays when cold and bagged when solid. It is then a relatively simple task to have a bowl of soup in a flash by placing the relevant number of cubes in a bowl and melting them over a saucepan of simmering water. (Don't place the cubes into a saucepan over direct heat or they will catch.)

The following is the *basic* recipe, so use it when making any of the other suggested soups. Each has 2 lb (900 g) prepared vegetables – peeled, scraped, topped and tailed etc, whatever is appropriate – and these are chopped into even-sized pieces. Each uses the butter, onions, sherry and stock in the same proportions, and then different flavourings and seasonings are added.

BASIC CREAM OF VEGETABLE SOUP

——— · • · ———

· serves 6–12 ·

4 oz (100 g) butter
8 oz (225 g) onions, peeled and finely chopped
2 lb (900 g) prepared and chopped vegetables
5 fl oz (150 ml) cooking sherry
1½–2 pints (900 ml–1.2 litres) good home-made stock
salt and freshly ground black pepper

Melt the butter in a large pan and cook the chopped onions until soft and golden. Add the prepared vegetables and stir around until coated with the buttery onion. Pour in the sherry – at this stage, some other flavourings are often added – and cover closely with a dampened, doubled sheet of greaseproof paper. Leave to simmer gently, preferably covered with the pan lid, for 40–45 minutes; the veg *make* moisture, but do check from time to time that they're not catching on the bottom of the pan.

After this time, add the stock, and then liquidise the soup in batches. Pass each liquidised batch through a sieve into a clean pan.

Reheat very gently, and taste for seasoning. Add salt and pepper if necessary and any other flavouring or garnishing.

I like to use cold, raw, finely chopped contrasting vegetables and fruits for garnishing soups. It may sound strange putting 3 dessert gooseberries into a bowl of Calvados apple chive soup, but it isn't as far as I am concerned. A carrot and caraway soup can be garnished with finely chopped pineapple, and very thin banana circles and toasted almonds are lovely on a cream of nutmeg spinach soup. Likewise celery and mustard soup looks good with finely chopped red or green peppers. You could also enrich and decorate by simply pouring in a little twirl of cream or natural yoghurt. And, of course, you could use croûtons, plain or slightly fancier, see below.

Soup Variations

MUSHROOM AND BACON

2 lb (900 g) mushrooms, trimmed

for the garnish
4 oz (100 g) cooked bacon dice

You can serve the soup chilled, in which case use 1½ pints (900 ml) stock.

CELERY AND GARDEN PEAS

1 lb (450 g) celery, trimmed, strings removed
1 lb (450 g) garden peas

for the garnish
a small celery twirl (p. 131) or a few raw peas

To serve chilled, reduce the stock quantity as above.

CARROT AND PARSNIP

1 lb (450 g) carrots, scrubbed and trimmed
1 lb (450 g) parsnips, scrubbed and trimmed

for the garnish
croûtons (see below) or some lightly curried leek rings (p. 127)

PORT AND MUSHROOM

2 lb (900 g) mushrooms
10 fl oz (300 ml) inexpensive port

for the garnish
1 oz (25 g) toasted flaked almonds

Use 1½ pints (900 ml) *milk* instead of stock, and add the port when simmering the mushrooms with the onions. Serve warm or very cold.

CARROT AND CARAWAY

2 lb (900 g) carrots, scrubbed and trimmed
2 tablespoons caraway seeds
2 tablespoons caster sugar

for the garnish
fineley chopped fresh pineapple

CALVADOS, APPLE AND CHIVE

2 lb (900 g) dessert apples
2 oz (50 g) chives
Calvados to taste

for the garnish
finely chopped fresh chives, or raw dessert gooseberries

Add the Calvados to taste when reheating the soup.

NUTMEG AND SPINACH

2 lb (900 g) fresh spinach, washed and thick stalks removed
1 whole nutmeg, freshly grated

for the garnish
very thin banana circles and toasted flaked almonds

Add the nutmeg when reheating the soup.

CELERY AND MUSTARD

2 lb (900 g) celery, trimmed, strings removed
3 tablespoons dry English mustard powder
1 tablespoon caster sugar

for the garnish
mustard and cress, or small sprigs of watercress

Soup Croûtons

All cream soups are enhanced by croûtons but, yes, I do agree, they are a fag to make at the last moment. Now, if you follow my advice, they can be made in advance and cooked fresh just before serving. When you get to the end of any loaf use the remains for croûtons. Slice the bread, remove the crusts and then carefully cut to the shape of cubed croûtons. Lay them flat on a roasting tray and when the oven is being used for other cooking simply put the tray in for 5–15 minutes (according to temperature), turning now and then to literally dry them out and make them quite hard. When cold put in a screw-top jar and keep in the fridge for up to a week. When you need hot, crunchy, crisp croûtons for soup, simply fry off the desired quantity in equal parts of olive oil and butter over a medium heat.

Cheese Croûton Triangles

These are admirable served straight from the oven with cream soups, but they're just as nice cold.

· *makes 12 triangles* ·

6 bread slices
4 oz (100 g) Parmesan cheese, grated
2 oz (50 g) soft butter
1 egg yolk
1 teaspoon mustard of choice
a pinch of salt

Pre-heat the oven to gas mark 4, 350°F (180°C).

Do not remove the crusts from the bread. Toast well on one side only. Mix the remaining ingredients together well and spread on the untoasted side of the bread. Bake for 20 minutes in the pre-heated oven, then remove crusts. Cut the slices into triangles.

Puff Pastry Rounds

These are ideal for picnics, but they can be served fresh and hot from the oven at a supper. The various fillings are in roughly 12 oz (350 g) quantities: these will fill six rounds. There will be pastry left over, and if you want to make *more* rounds, simply increase the filling in proportion.

· *makes 1 lb (450 g) puff pastry* ·

1 lb (450 g) strong plain flour
a generous pinch of salt
8 oz (225 g) each of soft margarine and lard or shortening,
broken up into $\frac{1}{2}$ oz (15 g) pieces
1 tablespoon lemon juice made up to 10 fl oz (300 ml) with
very cold water

to finish
1 egg, beaten with a little cold water
filling of choice, see below

Sieve the flour and salt into a bowl. Put in the margarine and lard and shake to coat the fat with flour. Make a well in the centre and pour in the measured liquid. Mix roughly with a palette knife.

Flour your work-top well and turn the dough out of the bowl, scraping off anything stuck to the sides. Pat roughly to the shape of a brick, short end nearest you. Holding the rolling pin at both ends, delicately tap the brick in the middle and at the top and bottom. Then, starting at the rolling pin impression nearest you, give the rolling pin a good push and a slight downward pressure. Do not *press* down, but make sharp, soft movements away from you until the pastry slowly and gradually becomes a rectangle measuring roughly 16 × 5 in (40 × 12 cm).

Fold this rectangle into three equal parts, bringing the bottom third up over the middle third, and then the top third down on to the other two thirds. To trap the air between these layers tap down lightly with the rolling pin on to the open sides at left and right, and in front of you. Give the dough a quarter turn – turn it from 6 to 9 o'clock – and put to one side for about 5 minutes.

The pastry will be slightly easier to handle now. Repeat the tapping, turning, rolling, folding and resting process three more times, generously flouring the board or work-top between each rolling so that the dough does not stick. Simply brush off the surplus (I use a paintbrush). On the fourth and final rolling, the dough may be a little resistant, so don't *force* it into the 16×5 inch (40×12 cm) shape. Pop into a polythene bag and chill overnight.

Never start to roll the pastry until it comes back to a workable consistency after taking it from the fridge, about 20–30 minutes in a warm kitchen.

Flour your work-top and rolling pin well. Turn the slab of pastry so that the C shape of the folded-over bottom third (from the last folding) is nearest you, then roll out to about $\frac{1}{8}$ in (3 mm) thickness. Cut out 12×4 in (10 cm) circles with a cutter and lay 6 of these flat on your work-top. Paint the rims with the mixture of beaten egg and cold water. Spoon on to this round 2 oz (50 g) of your chosen filling, then place the other circle on top. Using a fork, secure the edge to the egg-painted part of the bottom circle. Paint all over with the egg mix, then leave to chill in the fridge for 30 minutes.

Pre-heat the oven to gas mark 6, 400°F (200°C) and place the rounds on a dampened baking tray. Bake in the oven for 15–20 minutes. Eat warm, or leave to go cold.

SALMON, EGG AND RICE

Mix 8 oz (225 g) canned salmon (or tuna) with 2 shelled hard-boiled eggs, coarsely chopped, and 2 oz (50 g) cooked rice.

BEEF, ONION AND WALNUT

Fry 2 oz (50 g) chopped onions in 1 oz (25 g) butter and 1 tablespoon olive oil, then add 8 oz (225 g) well seasoned minced beef and 6 coarsely chopped walnuts.

PORK, ONION AND PINEAPPLE

Fry 2 oz (50 g) chopped onions in 1 oz (25 g) butter and 1 tablespoon olive oil, then add 8 oz (225 g) seasoned minced pork and 2 oz (50 g) finely chopped fresh pineapple.

SWEETCORN, CHEESE AND CHUTNEY

For vegetarians, mix 8 oz (225 g) sweetcorn with 4 oz (100 g) coarsely grated Cheddar cheese and a little chutney.

VEAL OLIVES

——— · • · ———

This, like the potted spiced salmon on p. 44, was adapted from a seventeenth-century cookery book, and published in the tercentenary issue of *Lloyd's Log*. It's delicious served hot with the ginger sauce given below, but it can also be eaten cold, taken in its cling film wrapping on a picnic.

Escalopes of veal can be bought ready prepared, and usually weigh between 5–6 oz (150–175 g) each, but it is very easy as well as considerably cheaper to cut them yourself from a bought cushion of veal. Cut the slices at an angle across the grain. Start the preparation of both escalopes and filling the day before you want to serve.

· serves 6 ·

6 veal escalopes
10 fl oz (300 ml) dry white wine
butter

for the filling
8 oz (225 g) raw chicken breast, cubed
2 eggs
5 fl oz (150 ml) double cream
6 spinach or sorrel leaves, washed and stalks removed
1 tablespoon parsley heads
2 fresh sage leaves
salt and freshly ground black pepper

for the sauce (if used)
6 black peppercorns
1 pint (600 ml) double cream
$\frac{1}{2}$ teaspoon salt
2–3 pieces preserved ginger

Place the escalopes in a large shallow dish and cover with the wine. Put cling film over and leave in the fridge for 24 hours. Put the cubed chicken for the filling into the food processor and blend, adding the eggs one at a time. Leave this mixture in the fridge for the same length of time.

The next day, pre-heat the oven to gas mark 4, 350°F (180°C). Return the chicken-egg mixture to the processor and blend in the cream, spinach or sorrel and herbs, plus a generous pinch of salt and some freshly ground black pepper.

To prepare the olives, lay out some squares of cling film (large enough to enclose the rolled escalopes), and coat generously on one side with butter. Remove the escalopes from the wine marinade (save the latter for the sauce if you're going to make it) and lay flat on the buttered cling film squares. Divide the filling between them, spread out, and roll up in the cling film, securely twisting the ends so that each escalope looks like a large wrapped boiled sweet.

Place the parcels on a cooling tray in a roasting tray, and pour enough hot water in to come up to the bottom of the cooling tray. Put in the pre-heated oven and cook for 35 minutes. Serve hot with the sauce below, or carry in the cling film to eat cold on a picnic.

To make the sauce, put the veal wine marinade into a pan, add the peppercorns, then boil briskly to reduce by half. Meanwhile, put the cream in a deep heavy pan with the salt and simmer over a very low heat until this too is reduced by half (about 45 minutes). Put the ginger in the liquidiser, then pour on the reduced cream and sieved wine, blend, and lo and behold, a delicious sauce!

CHICKEN BREAST STUFFED WITH BANANA AND MANGO, BAKED IN SMOKED BACON

—— · · ——

If serving this for supper or dinner at home, unwrap each breast from the foil before taking to the table, but it's ideal picnic fodder, delicious cold, and already wrapped for transportation.

· *serves 6* ·

butter
6 boned chicken breasts
1 medium fresh mango, peeled and cut into 6 wedges
$1\frac{1}{2}$ bananas, peeled, halved lengthwise and then cut in two
6 large smoked bacon rashers, rinded
white wine

to serve
hollandaise (p. 159) (optional)

Pre-heat the oven to gas mark 4, 350°F (180°C), and butter 6 pieces of foil large enough to enclose the breasts. Do this on the *dull* side of the foil.

Put the breasts, skin side down, on your work surface and make an incision about 2 in (5 cm) long into the flesh underneath the fillet. This must be big enough to take a small wedge of mango and a piece of banana. Insert the mango first, and the banana on top. Fold the fillet over to close.

Lay the smoked bacon rashers down on your work surface and place each chicken breast, fillet side down, on the fat end of the bacon. Wrap the thin tail bit of the bacon round the chicken.

Place each wrapped breast on a piece of buttered foil. Start to bring the four sides of the foil up so that when you pour in about 1 tablespoon white wine per parcel, it does not run all over your work surface. Place a knob of butter on each breast. Secure the foil carefully all round to form the shape of a Cornish pasty, making doubly sure the wine won't be able to run out. Place these parcels on a wire cooling tray placed in a roasting tray. Fill this latter with some hot water and place the whole thing in the pre-heated oven. Cook for 30 minutes.

BAKED BANANAS WITH BUTTERSCOTCH SAUCE

First of all let me say that this butterscotch sauce is something everybody should have in their fridge stored in a screw-top jar as it comes in so handy for unexpected guests – and for adding that extra something to the simplest basic, a piece of sponge cake or a baked banana as here. It can keep in the fridge for 10–14 days.

If you want to barbecue the bananas, wrap them individually in foil and leave over the coals for about 10–15 minutes. Or take them on a picnic wrapped in foil after baking at home, with the sauce in a screw-top jar. Remember spoons, and all guests have to do is unwrap the foil, spoon into the slit in the blackened skins of the bananas, and enjoy the mushy flesh with a little sauce.

· *serves 6* ·

6 reasonably ripe bananas

Butterscotch sauce
3 oz (75 g) soft butter
4 oz (100 g) soft brown sugar
3 oz (75 g) granulated sugar
1 lb (450 g) golden syrup
5 fl oz (150 ml) double cream
a few drops of vanilla essence

Make the sauce up to 4–5 days beforehand, and keep in the fridge. Put the butter, sugars and syrup in a large pan and heat gently. When they have all come together, simply continue to cook for a further 10 minutes, stirring from time to time with a wooden spoon. Remove from the heat and beat in the double cream with some vanilla essence. When cool, put in the jar.

To bake the bananas in the oven, pre-heat to gas mark 4, 350° F (180° C). Make an incision two-thirds of the way down one side of each banana, and put on a baking sheet. Bake for about 10–20 minutes, but so much depends on how ripe they were in the first place. Leave to cool then wrap in foil to take on a picnic.

BLENDER CHEESECAKES

——— · • · ———

Heavier than others I've done in the past? Yes. But easier? Decidedly and definitely! In fact I really do like the texture, and what I do, because the texture is *denser,* is to put *two* different mixes into each cheesecake. So, not only do they look interesting and tempting, they also titillate the palate – and by now you will have realised how much I enjoy doing this! By using your blender for this dish it means that you cut down tremendously on the washing up, and that's another important factor as far as I am concerned.

Take the whole cheesecake in its tin to a picnic wrapped securely in foil. The recipe will give you 6 piggish portions, 8 large portions, or 12 normal portions to finish a meal.

for the base
1 × 10 oz (275 g) packet chocolate digestive biscuits
2 oz (50 g) butter, melted

for the filling
(use *twice* this, with different flavourings)
$\frac{1}{2}$ oz (15 g) powdered gelatine
5 tablespoons alcohol (see below)
9 oz (250 g) good cream cheese
2 whole eggs plus 2 egg yolks
2 oz (50 g) caster sugar
10 fl oz (300 ml) double cream
flavouring of choice (see below)

Pre-heat the oven to gas mark 4, 350° F (180° C) and line a 10 in (25 cm) loose-bottomed, spring-sided cake tin with good greaseproof paper.

For the base, drop the biscuits in pieces into your liquidiser and reduce to fine crumbs. Turn out into a mixing bowl, add the melted butter and mix to a dough paste consistency. Put this over the base of the prepared tin, and bake in the pre-heated oven for 15 minutes. Remove and leave to cool. The cooling is most important or else, when you add your cheesecake mixture, you will end up with a peculiar and soggy base!

As I said, because this blender mix is much denser than the norm, use two times the filling quantity above, flavouring them differently according to choice from the alternatives below, and put one on top of the other. (So, to make *one* cheesecake, you'll need 18 oz/500 g cream cheese etc.)

First of all, put the gelatine into a small saucepan, and pour the desired liquid in *all in one go* – here 5 tablespoons of an alcohol (see below). Gently swirl the pan around until the fine particles dissolve and become rather tacky; put to one side and leave until reconstitution time comes around.

While this is happening, put the cream cheese, eggs and egg yolks, sugar and cream into the food processor with the flavouring of choice – see below – and mix to a cream.

To reconstitute the gelatine, put the gelatine pan on the *very lowest heat* possible. Keep feeling the bottom of the pan with your hand; it shouldn't hurt, *that's* how low! The gelatine will be reconstituted to a clear liquid, and then you pour or dribble it into your mixture through a warmed metal sieve (warmed so that the gelatine won't stick to the mesh on a cold day). For this blender cheesecake, dribble the gelatine into the blender while it is going; for non-blender gelatine mixtures, fold the gelatine in well, using a long-handled spoon in a figure-of-eight motion.

Pour the first cheesecake mix into the paper- and biscuit-lined tin, and leave to set. Make up the second mix and pour on top of the first. Most dishes with gelatine require 6–8 hours in the fridge to be ready for serving (although smaller containers will probably set quicker). Garnish the cheesecake after taking out of the tin with twirls of cream and/or some appropriate fruits.

CHEESECAKE FLAVOURINGS

——— ·•· ———

STRAWBERRY

Use 8 oz (225 g) strawberries, hulled, and reconstitute the gelatine with brandy.

RASPBERRY

Use 8 oz (225 g) raspberries, hulled, and reconstitute the gelatine with Kirsch.

COFFEE AND RUM

Use 2 tablespoons Camp Coffee and reconstitute the gelatine with dark rum. If you like, you can add 4 oz (100 g) chopped pecan nuts.

BANANA RUM

Use 2 large ripe bananas, roughly chopped, and reconstitute the gelatine with dark rum.

ORANGE HAZELNUT

Use the juice and finely grated rind of 2 oranges, and 3 oz (75 g) ground hazelnuts. Reconstitute the gelatine with orange curaçao.

LEMON

Use the juice and finely grated rind of 2 lemons, and reconstitute the gelatine with gin.

GOOSEBERRY

Use 8 oz (225 g) dessert gooseberries, trimmed, and reconstitute the gelatine with gin.

CHOCOLATE

Use 5 oz (150 g) good chocolate melted with 2 tablespoons rum, and reconstitute the gelatine with rum.

HONEY AND LEMON FLAN

This combination of sweet and sour flavours encased in the rich light pastry is ideal for a picnic if transported in its container. Remember to have a tin or something to balance the base on while you slip off the side of the flan tin.

· serves 8 ·

1 × 10 in (25 cm) sweet wheatmeal pastry flan case, baked
blind (p. 33)
1 lb (450 g) good cream cheese
4 oz (100 g) caster sugar
2 tablespoons runny honey
6 eggs, lightly beaten
juice and finely grated rind of 2 lemons
freshly grated nutmeg (optional)

Pre-heat the oven to gas mark 3, 325° F (160° C). Place the flan case ready on a baking tray.

Cream the cheese with the sugar then beat in the runny honey. Little by little beat in the lightly beaten eggs, followed by the lemon juice and rind. (If you are a fan, freshly grated nutmeg may be added to the filling before you put it in the oven.) Pour this mixture into the pastry case and bake in the pre-heated oven for 45 minutes. Leave to cool.

CINNAMON COOKIES

Make the dough the day before you want to bake and serve the biscuits, for morning coffee, afternoon tea or a crisp finale to a picnic meal.

Make the little rabbit and hedgehog biscuits for a children's tea from this mixture, but use ginger instead of cinnamon. Or you could divide the mixture in two, flavouring half with cinnamon, half with ground ginger.

· makes 70 tiny biscuits ·

10 oz (275 g) self-raising flour
4 oz (100 g) caster sugar
4 oz (100 g) soft butter
2 teaspoons ground cinnamon
2 egg yolks
5 tablespoons double cream
1 egg, beaten (optional)

Put the flour, sugar, butter, cinnamon and egg yolks into your mixer bowl, and start working to a dough with the K beater. Add the cream, tablespoon by tablespoon, until you get a firm but smooth dough.

Roll out on to the *base* of a turned-over baking tray of 10 × 14 in (25 × 35 cm) which you have greased and lined with good greaseproof paper. Cover with another piece of greaseproof and leave overnight in the fridge.

The next day, pre-heat the oven to gas mark 4, 350°F (180°C), and mark the dough into 2 in (5 cm) squares, then into triangles. Brush with beaten egg if you want the biscuits to have a gloss, and bake in the pre-heated oven for 30 minutes. Turn the tray round after 15 minutes. Cut through completely along the lines before cold.

LEMON AND WALNUT BREAD

——— · • · ———

I call this a bread as it is made in a loaf tin, but it is really a cross between soft bread and a cornflour sponge in texture. Slice it thinly, and spread generously with soft butter.

· makes 1 × 2 lb (900 g) loaf ·

6 oz (175 g) soft butter
10 oz (275 g) caster sugar
4 eggs, lightly beaten
juice and finely grated rind of 2 lemons
10 oz (275 g) plain flour, sieved
1 teaspoon baking powder
2 oz (50 g) walnuts, finely chopped

for the syrup
5 oz (150 g) caster sugar
juice of 2 lemons

Pre-heat the oven to gas mark 4, 350°F (180°C), and grease, flour and sugar a 2 lb (900 g) loaf tin.

Cream the soft butter well with the caster sugar, and little by little add the beaten eggs, followed by the lemon rind and juice. Fold in the sieved plain flour and the baking powder along with the chopped walnuts.

Pour into the prepared loaf tin and bake in the pre-heated oven for $1\frac{1}{2}$ hours. There's no need to cover.

Remove from the oven and leave to cool slightly while you make the syrup. Melt the sugar with the lemon juice, and when it becomes a clear liquid, pour over the top of the bread. Leave overnight covered with foil. The loaf develops a sort of crystalline top.

Nutty Wholemeal Bread

I always use fresh yeast for this as I often find dried yeast leaves a flavour in the end product. Each winter when the staff and I travel on our cooking trips overseas, fresh yeast is the one ingredient we always take frozen. And on the residential cookery courses at Miller Howe held each spring and autumn, the smell of this bread baking during the Monday morning session is only made more pleasant by us eating it hot and doughy liberally spread with butter at lunch to accompany our cups of home-made carrot and coriander soup. Quite delicious, but *not* to be recommended as a daily habit!

I must admit the bread doesn't toast *evenly* for breakfast, but served with home-made marmalade it is a winner. The only disadvantage is that guests or family will double their normal morning consumption. It's also delicious used in sandwiches, spread liberally with butter. The addition of the oats gives it a crunch and flavour which is hard to beat, but you could add, instead of the oats, a couple of tablespoons of crushed dried banana flakes, or chopped hazelnuts, pecans or walnuts. Sultanas could be used too, and you could sprinkle caraway or sesame seeds on the top of the dough after it has risen.

· *makes 2 × 2 lb (900 g) loaves* ·

butter
1 lb (450 g) wholemeal flour
1 teaspoon salt
4 tablespoons Jordans original crunchy oats
2 tablespoons black treacle or runny honey mixed with
5 fl oz (150 ml) warm water
2 oz (50 g) fresh yeast
10 fl oz (300 ml) warm water

Lightly butter 2 loaf tins, and have 2 bowls, a large and medium size, at the ready. Place the flour, salt and oats in the larger bowl and put in a warm place – the oven with just the pilot light on, or an airing cupboard. Put the treacle or honey and water mixture into the second bowl and crumble the fresh yeast on top. Leave this in a warm place for up to 10 minutes until the yeast has formed a frothy head like an Irish stout.

Add the 10 fl oz (300 ml) warm water to the yeasty bowl, and then add the mixed liquid to the warmed flour bowl. Bring together with a long-handled spoon to form a dough.

Flour your hands and divide this sticky dough between the buttered tins, pressing it down well. Cover loosely with greaseproof paper and put the tins in a warm place for 20–30 minutes. The dough in the tins doubles in size.

Meanwhile pre-heat the oven to gas mark 6, 400°F (200°C).

Remove the greaseproof paper, put the tins in the pre-heated oven and bake for 40 minutes. It will sound hollow when patted on its bottom! Turn out on to a cooling tray and leave until cold (if you can resist!) before slicing. Keep for 10 days in the bread tin, 20 days, wrapped, in the fridge, or freeze.

CHAPTER FOUR

TEAS AND HIGH TEAS

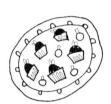

The stiffly starched tablecloth laid with the best china and cutlery (stored in the large sideboard of the living room) is a vivid memory of my childhood Sundays at my grandmother's house. It reeked of home baking and the table groaned with freshly made breads, buns, loaves, egg custards, pies, cakes and pastries. Toasted teacakes were prepared one by one on the end of an extending toasting fork held over the coal-burning fire in the living-room grate, and were always eaten with butter and generous slices of sharp white Lancashire cheese.

In summer a high tea would start off with cold meats and salad (mundane by modern expectations), and at other times of the year fried or baked fish, baked ham or Welsh rarebit were the order of the day, to be followed by the more conventional tea-time fare. There are a few ideas here that can be used for both teas and high teas, and indeed you'll find many recipes throughout the book that could be adapted for use at these meal times.

Children always seem to be associated with tea times and with cakes, cream and biscuits – although why, I wonder, as most children of my acquaintance seem to be rather keener on *savoury* items? – and so we concocted a few tea-time delicacies to celebrate those wonderful books written by Beatrix Potter. For more than 80 years now, the adventures of Peter Rabbit, Tom Kitten, Jemima Puddle-Duck, Mrs Tiggywinkle, and all their friends have captivated the imagination of children the whole world over, and it was the animals and countryside of the Lake District that inspired Beatrix Potter to create them.

MENU ONE

SMOKED HADDOCK AND EGG MOUSSE *91*

HAM BAKED WITH HONEY AND CIDER *92*

HAZELNUT CREAM WITH BANANAS AND
FRANGELICO *106*

———·•·———

MENU TWO

COLD SALMON STEAK WITH AVOCADO PURÉE AND
MAYONNAISE *93*

APPLE CHARLOTTES *104*
WITH HOT LEMON SAUCE *105*

———·•·———

SMOKED HADDOCK AND EGG MOUSSE

This makes a nice starter for a high tea or a supper.

· fills 8 ramekins ·

1 lb (450 g) smoked haddock on the bone
10 fl oz (300 ml) milk
1 bay leaf
4 black peppercorns
$\frac{1}{2}$ oz (15 g) gelatine
5 tablespoons white wine
4 tablespoons home-made mayonnaise (p. 56)
3 hard-boiled eggs, finely chopped
juice and finely grated rind of $\frac{1}{2}$ lemon
1 whole nutmeg, finely grated
5 fl oz (150 ml) double cream

for the garnish
thin cucumber slices
tiny watercress sprigs

Poach the smoked haddock, with skin and bone, in the milk along with the bay leaf and black peppercorns, for about 5 minutes. Drain well, discarding the flavoured milk, then remove and discard the haddock bones and skin. Put the gelatine in a small pan, pour in the wine in one go, and leave to one side (p. 79).

Put the haddock flesh in the food processor along with the mayonnaise and blend together. Turn out into a mixing bowl and mix in the chopped hard-boiled eggs, the lemon juice and rind and grated nutmeg. Lightly beat the double cream, and fold this into the mixture.

Reconstitute the gelatine in the wine as described on p. 79, and fold well into the mixture. Divide between the 8 ramekins, and leave to set in a cool place, about 2 hours.

Garnish with very thin slices of cucumber and in the middle put the very end sprig of watercress. Serve with slices of the wheatmeal bread on p. 84, made with honey.

Ham Baked with Honey and Cider

Sweet toothed as I am, this is an especial favourite, served with either peach wedges or a slice of fresh pineapple.

· *serves 6* ·

1 ham, about 6–8 lb (2.7–3.6 kg) in weight
6 tablespoons runny honey
about 30 cloves
$1\frac{1}{2}$ pints (900 ml) cider

The secret of tasty ham devoid of salt is to soak it for at least 4 days in a large pan completely covered with cold water from the tap, and to change the water first thing in the morning and last thing at night. Keep in the fridge or a cold place. Having done this, the ham can then be cooked.

After the final soaking, remove the ham, leaving the water in the pan. Put the pan on the hob, adding the honey, and bring to the boil. Replace the ham in this mixture, bring back to the boil and simmer away covered for 2 hours. Check the liquid level from time to time, but it shouldn't be necessary to add more. Remove the ham from the liquid and leave to cool.

With a sharp knife, remove the skin and then cut through the fat to make diamond shapes. Into each one of these you stick a clove.

When you want to roast, pre-heat the oven to gas mark 5, 375°F (190°C). Bring the cider to the boil, and pour into a roasting tray. Place the ham on top, and bake, basting every 15 minutes, for an hour. The ham can be served hot, but is equally delicious cold.

COLD SALMON STEAK WITH AVOCADO PURÉE AND MAYONNAISE

———··———

This is a relatively simple, but satisfying dish for a high tea. Needless to say, it would be quite suitable for a lunch or dinner main course too!

· *serves 6* ·

6 salmon steaks
1 ripe avocado
a few drops of lemon juice
5 fl oz (150 ml) blender mayonnaise (p. 57)

for the garnish
cucumber and radish slices
dill sprigs

Prepare and cook the salmon steaks as on p. 43 then allow to go cold. With a fish slice, transfer to your serving dishes.

Peel and stone the avocado, and then blend the flesh to a purée with the lemon juice. Spread this purée over one half of each cold salmon steak, the mayonnaise over the other. Place 3 very thin slices of scored cucumber down the middle and, if you have the patience and time, top with 3 very thin circles of radish and a sprig of dill. An alternative garnish could be radish flowers (p. 131) on hard-boiled egg rounds along with sprigs of parsley or mint.

BAKED STUFFED AVOCADO WRAPPED IN BACON

—— ·•· ——

This makes a delicious starter to a meal, or a light lunch, high tea or supper on its own – a change from the raw half filled with vinaigrette or prawns.

· per person ·

½ avocado pear
about ½ oz (15 g) toasted sesame seeds
1 oz (25 g) cheese and herb pâté (p. 38)
2 smoked bacon rashers, rinded

Pre-heat the oven to gas mark 4, 350°F (180°C).

Skin the pear half, then roll in sesame seeds. Pipe or spoon the cheese and herb pâté into the hole in each avocado half and then generously wrap in the bacon rashers. Place the avocado, filling side down, on a baking tray and bake in the pre-heated oven for about 10 minutes. Finish off under the grill to further brown the bacon if necessary.

LEMON SLICE

—··—

This has a very unusual texture, half-way between a biscuit and a sponge, but the lemon cream is what makes it so moreish.

· makes 1 × 3-tier 8 in (20 cm) gâteau ·

6 eggs, separated
2 tablespoons warm water
6 oz (175 g) caster sugar
juice and finely grated rind of 2 lemons
3 oz (75 g) plain flour
1 oz (25 g) cornflour

for the filling and topping
1 egg
5 oz (150 g) caster sugar
juice and finely grated rind of 1 lemon
2 tablespoons dry white wine
1 oz (25 g) plain flour
10 fl oz (300 ml) double cream

Pre-heat the oven to gas mark 4, 350°F (180°C), and grease, sugar and flour 3 × 8 in (20 cm) sponge tins.

Warm your mixer bowl and beat the egg yolks with the warm water until light and fluffy (about 10 minutes). Beat in the sugar a little at a time. When it has all been mixed in, beat in the warmed lemon juice and rind drop by drop. Sieve the flour and cornflour together and fold into the mixture.

Divide between the prepared tins and bake in the pre-heated oven for 45 minutes. Remove and leave to cool before turning out.

To make the filling/topping, beat the egg with the sugar and lemon rind and juice mixture along with the wine, then beat in the plain flour. Cook in a bowl over a pan of simmering water until it thickens, stirring continuously (about 15 minutes). Leave to go cold, then pass through a sieve and combine with the cream. Beat to soft peak texture.

To assemble the 'slice', build up the three circles with two layers of the flavoured cream, then spread the balance of the cream over the top and sides. Use a fork to give a rough plastered effect.

Mr McGregor's Garden or Carrot and Nut Cake

—··—

Not being a family man, it used to be tricky thinking of dishes that I could prepare for the children of friends. Now I find that most kids will eat (or attempt to eat) anything, particularly if it *looks* interesting. This cake – which can, of course, be decorated in any way you like – fulfils all these requirements, being interesting to look at for children, but it's quite delicious to eat, for both kids and adults. It could even be served as a dessert.

· *makes 1 × 4-tiered 10 in (25 cm) cake* ·

melted butter
ground hazelnuts
12 oz (350 g) peeled and finely grated carrots, left for 30 minutes in a sieve (push occasionally to get rid of excess liquid)
4 oz (100 g) hazelnuts, finely chopped
2 oz (50 g) walnuts, finely chopped
3 oz (75 g) ground almonds
1 teaspoon baking powder
$\frac{1}{4}$ teaspoon freshly grated nutmeg
6 eggs, separated
6 oz (175 g) caster sugar, sieved

for the filling and topping
1 lb (450 g) good cream cheese
10 fl oz (300 ml) double cream
4 tablespoons caster sugar

for the decoration
cocoa powder, sieved
rabbit biscuits (p. 82)
Matchmakers
angelica
minute carrot 'carrots', with dill fronds

Pre-heat the oven to gas mark 4, 350°F (180°C), and line 2 × 10 in (25 cm) round spring-sided cake tins with good greaseproof or Bakewell paper. Paint the sides with melted butter and scatter over some ground hazelnuts.

Combine the drained carrots, hazelnuts, walnuts, almonds, baking powder and nutmeg in a large bowl.

In a warmed mixer bowl, beat the egg yolks until light and fluffy then, gradually, beat in the sugar. Gently fold into the dry ingredients.

Wash the mixer bowl, finish it off with cold water and wipe dry, then beat the egg whites until stiff like a meringue mix. Fold half into the mixture, leaving the rest beating away on the machine. Fold the balance in, and divide the mixture between the prepared tins. Bake in the pre-heated oven for 1 hour. Remove from the oven and when cooling remove from the tins and put on cooling trays.

When cold, slit each cake in half horizontally so you will then have 3 layers to fill and a top to decorate. For the filling and topping, beat together the cream cheese and cream and fold in the sugar. Spread 3 of the circles with the filling, leaving enough to cover the sides and top, and place one on top of the other.

To decorate the cake, you can really do what you like. As Beatrix Potter lived in the Lake District, we chose to represent Mr McGregor's garden (after a fashion): the cream cheese topping was furrowed and then dusted with sifted cocoa powder to look like a ploughed field. The furrows were planted with minute carrot 'carrots' and dill carrot fronds – a labour of love and patience, this – and lettuces made from soaked angelica. The garden is surrounded by some Flopsy Bunny biscuits trying to get through the Matchmaker fence.

SCONES

When making scones, it is important that you take time and trouble to weigh out the ingredients accurately, and as far as scales are concerned, I always use the old-fashioned pan-balance ones which will weigh down to the last quarter ounce. (Plastic spring-balanced ones can't do this, particularly when they get older as the spring balances weaken.) Never store your weights *on* the pan, though, but keep them in a pyramid high on the work surface. Being a messy cook I find I often have to wash the weights, and when I dry them I put them in a cooling oven to dry off completely to avoid them rusting.

Light scones can only be made when you feel light-hearted. It is no use getting everything out and ready for scone-making if your innate irritability will reveal itself in the butter and flour mixing, and thus in ultimately heavy scones. Once you have mastered the technique and the recipe, you can experiment with flavourings for the basic scones. Instead of the sultanas and sugar you could use grated Cheddar cheese and a spice such as ground coriander; you could add curry powder, ground ginger or cinnamon, grated orange or lemon peel, cracked dried banana flakes, chopped prunes or apricots, ground nuts. . . .

· *makes 16–20 scones* ·

1 lb (450 g self-raising flour, sieved
a pinch of salt
6 oz (175 g) soft butter, cut into pieces
3 tablespoons caster sugar, sieved
4 oz (100 g) sultanas
2 eggs, lightly beaten
milk, soured cream or natural yoghurt to mix

Pre-heat the oven to gas mark 7, 425°F (220°C), and line 2 baking trays with good greaseproof paper.

Use a large round-bottomed mixing bowl, and sieve the self-raising flour and salt into it. (Get into the habit of constantly sieving flour whenever cooking.) Get your butter really soft: this is essential, otherwise you will have to work hard at getting it rubbed into the flour. The object of the exercise is to coerce this butter into the flour as lightly as possible, allowing as much air as possible to get into the mix. In fact, before you start, as silly as it might sound, go in front of a mirror and keep bringing your outstretched hands together and then bring them up making larger and larger outward circles; as you bring them up, spread open the fingers and lightly bring the thumbs across the four fingers on each hand, never actually touching them. This will mean the soft butter will spread into the flour, dropping between your open fingers. The light movement might seem lengthy, but the resultant evenly distributed butter means successful scones. Apply this same movement to the ingredients in the bowl.

Distribute the sugar and sultanas gently with your finger tips and put the eggs on top of the mixture, with a little of the milk, soured cream or yoghurt.

The bowl should be held now at a 45 degree angle off the work surface with your non-work hand, and the other hand simply scoops (not squeezing) into the mixture, bringing it to the top of the bowl and allowing it to fall back again to the bottom (rather like a mechanical cement mixer churning away). Add a little more milk if necessary, but take care; if you added all the liquid or too much with the eggs, you could end up with a runny sponge-like mix rather than the desired one. As I do not know how large your eggs are, how creamy your butter is or how warm your hands are, you'll have to take all these into consideration yourself when judging the amount of liquid needed. You would never add the same amount of liquid two days running!

The scone dough should eventually be quite firmly bound. Having got this far many people then undo all the good work as they turn the dough out on to the floured work surface and, using the largest, heaviest rolling pin available, attack the mix like a steam-roller flattening and smoothing tarmac. No, no, *no*. Gently pat it out to the desired thickness – about an inch (2.5 cm) – and lightly press the sides in to make it a firm square shape. I never use scone cutters as these, whilst providing nice round, even and circular scones, make the scones slightly heavier at the edge by the forceful downward movement of the cutter (and of course you then have to scoop up the remnants and pat them down again to use up all the dough). Far better, with a large palette knife, to cut clear diagonal lines across and through the dough: the resultant rough diamonds are your finished scones.

Transfer to the lined baking tray and bake in the pre-heated oven for about 10 minutes. Take off the tray and cool on a cooling rack or eat hot. (If you wish to freeze the scones, do so raw on the open trays, and when frozen transfer to plastic bags and secure with tietags. Defrost before baking.)

Eat the sweet scones with jam and cream or with lime curd (p. 18), and the savoury ones make very good bases for cold meats, like ham, with pickles. I made some very good scones the other day with some Stilton and sage; they made a delicious 'Eggs Benedict', with a couple of poached eggs and some hollandaise (p. 159).

HAZELNUT MACAROONS

The circles can be stuck together with a coffee-flavoured butter cream or with whipped plain or flavoured double cream, or can be used in the sweet on p. 106.

· makes 24 biscuits ·

4 oz (100 g) egg whites (approx. 4 eggs)
6 oz (175 g) soft brown sugar
2 oz (50 g) caster sugar
2 oz (50 g) ground hazelnuts

Pre-heat the oven to gas mark 3, 325°F (160°C), and line two trays of about 15 × 11 in (38 × 28 cm) with good greaseproof paper.

Beat the egg whites until stiff and then little by little beat in the two mixed sugars. Fold in the ground hazelnuts.

Using 2 dessertspoons, spoon out dollops of the mixture on to the lined trays, leaving plenty of space around each one to allow for spreading. Bake for 1 hour in the pre-heated oven, then turn the oven off, prop the door open, and leave to cool.

Banana Gingerbread

——— · • · ———

Try to make this a couple of days before you eat it. It gets better as it 'ages'. Slice and spread generously with soft butter.

· makes 1 × 1 lb (450 g) loaf ·

8 oz (225 g) self-raising flour, sieved
a pinch of salt
1 heaped dessertspoon ground ginger
5 fl oz (150 ml) warm milk
4 oz (100 g) demerara sugar
3 oz (75 g) soft butter
5 fl oz (150 ml) black treacle
2 tablespoons golden syrup
3 ripe bananas, peeled and mashed
2 eggs, beaten

Pre-heat the oven to gas mark 3, 325°F (160°C), and grease and lightly flour a 1 lb (450 g) loaf tin.

Sieve the flour, salt and ginger into a large mixing bowl. Put the milk, sugar, butter, treacle and syrup into a saucepan and heat through – do not allow to boil. Beat in the mashed bananas and beaten eggs. (A couple of tablespoons of finely crushed dried banana flakes may also be added to the mixture.)

Make a well in the middle of your dry ingredients and pour the liquid mixture into this. Quickly combine to make a dough. Pour into the prepared loaf tin and bake in the pre-heated oven for $1\frac{1}{4}$ hours.

The loaf is best if it is turned out of the tin as it is cooling, wrapped in a double thickness of foil, and left for at least 3 days in an airtight tin before eating.

SUMMER FRUIT SPONGES

—— ·•· ——

If you spend a little extra time making these, you will soon have a rich texture that is as light as a feather. My grandmother used to pains-takingly make sponges in a chipped enamel bowl, using only her hand to beat and beat away (oh, what a labour of love in those days before mixers, electric whisks and processors), and although they were always ethereal in texture, they had a slightly sharp taste. I discovered why when I read her handwritten recipe books – she not only used self-raising flour but some baking powder as well. The latter is sharp in taste, but of course is an excellent rising agent.

Use any summer fruit you wish, or have a surplus of. You can use raspberries, wild Alpine strawberries or any of the currants whole, but dessert gooseberries quartered and large strawberries cut up into small segments are all excellent. A mixture is possible too, and blackberries could be used in season.

· makes 12 small sponges ·

4 oz (100 g) soft butter
4 oz (100 g) caster sugar
4 oz (100 g) eggs, weighed out of their shells (about 2 eggs)
4 oz (100 g) self-raising flour, sieved
4 oz (100 g) summer fruits (see above)

for the filling
jam, whipped flavoured cream, icing sugar

Pre-heat the oven to gas mark 4, 350°F (180°C), and place little paper cake cases in the holes in patty tins.

Place the soft butter in a round mixing bowl and add the sugar. Personally I feel that the heat of one's work hand is pretty useful to get these two started on their way, and you can be as rough as you like at this stage – just make sure the texture becomes creamy. Then, using an electric hand whisk, beat away at this mixture until it really is white, light and fluffy. You cannot *overdo* it but most people *under*beat, trying to get this stage over as quickly as possible, not realising just how important it is.

Beat the eggs together quite well – *never* break them one at a time on to the mix with the yolk and albumen visible. To add the egg, stop beating, and spread 1 tablespoon of the beaten egg all over the mix. Put the whisk on at top speed and beat until there is not a single sign of the egg left. Add a little more egg, in the same way, and continue doing this until all the egg is incorporated. If you are a trifle hasty at this stage, your mixture could curdle, and this will be quite obvious to your own two eyes. Don't give up and lose heart, simply stop beating, and add a tablespoon or two of the flour through the sieve. Fold in, using a large spoon, then add a little more of the egg mixture. Fold this in with the large spoon and go on until all the egg is used up.

When all the egg has been beaten in, sieve and fold in the flour, followed by the selected summer fruits. *Very carefully* bring the mixture all together so that the fruit is evenly distributed.

Use 2 dessertspoons to portion the mixture out into the paper cases, one to scoop it up and the other to drop it off! Put the trays in the pre-heated oven and bake for about 20 minutes. When the cakes come out of the oven, leave them for about 20–30 minutes in their containers and then remove – with their paper still on – to a cooling tray. At this stage I cannot resist the temptation to eat one warm, but ideally they should be served cold, filled with whipped and lightly flavoured cream (vanilla sugar – sugar stored with a vanilla pod to flavour it – is good for this).

To prepare them for filling, use a large Parisian scoop to scoop out the top and some of the middle, or insert a small sharp knife into the middle of the cake, turn it round and cut out a pyramid shape. Put this to one side. Pipe the whipped flavoured cream into this hole (you can have put the merest touch of home-made jam in the bottom) and then replace the pyramid of cake on top of the cream. Shower the whole delight with icing sugar.

APPLE CHARLOTTES

These delicious puddings go down very well (and extremely quickly) on a cold night, but are equally popular on other occasions, particularly when served with the following hot lemon sauce. Commercial dariole moulds will give you a better end result – resembling a small light-house – but to avoid the expense of buying these, 6 ramekins can be used for a flatter and rounder version. The taste doesn't alter with the shape!

· serves 6 ·

1 × sponge recipe (p. 102), minus the summer fruits
4 Granny Smith apples, peeled, cored and thinly sliced
2 tablespoons sweet cider

Pre-heat the oven to gas mark 4, 350°F (180°C), and lightly grease your 6 containers with some extra butter.

Make up the sponge as described on p. 102. Meanwhile, cook the apple slices in the cider until quite soft and then liquidise and pass through a sieve.

Divide two-thirds of the pudding mix between the chosen greased containers. With a teaspoon edge the mix up the sides and all over the base (it will look like a tartlet case) and then divide the apple mix between these indentations, filling the top with the balance of the sponge mix.

Place the containers on a baking sheet, and put in the pre-heated oven. Bake for 15–20 minutes until lightly browned. Remove from the oven and leave to rest for about 5 minutes before turning them out and serving them with a generous dollop of Calvados-flavoured whipped cream, a home-made vanilla custard or the following lemon sauce.

HOT LEMON SAUCE

This is nice served with any steamed pudding, and is different from regular custard. It is particularly good with the apple charlottes above. It can be made ahead of time and reheated without any problem.

· makes 10 fl oz (300 ml) ·

1 heaped tablespoon cornflour
3 tablespoons caster sugar, sieved
juice and finely grated rind of 2 lemons
10 fl oz (300 ml) milk, boiled with a generous knob of butter
3 egg yolks, gently beaten

Put the cornflour, sugar, lemon rind and juice into a Pyrex bowl and beat together. Place the bowl over a pan of simmering water, and add the boiled milk and melted butter through a sieve.

Beat in the egg yolks and continue to cook over the simmering water for about 10 minutes, stirring occasionally, until the mixture begins to thicken.

HAZELNUT CREAM WITH BANANAS AND FRANGELICO

———— · • · ————

Here is a pudding that will take minutes to assemble and will invariably go down well with guests as it is so rich and yummy.

· *serves 6* ·

10 fl oz (300 ml) double cream
2 tablespoons Frangelico (hazelnut liqueur)
2 tablespoons caster sugar
3 bananas, peeled and thinly sliced
6 hazelnut macaroons (p. 100), broken up

Beat the cream with the Frangelico and sugar to a stiff consistency, then fold in the bananas and hazelnut macaroons. Spoon out into saucer-shaped champagne glasses or Manhattan cocktail glasses on doyleyed plates.

A little grated chocolate and nutmeg on top with a sprig of fresh mint sets it off, and if cherries are in season, a few pairs on each serving plate will make the dish look even prettier.

Opposite: For a children's tea in celebration of Beatrix Potter, make a carrot and nut cake (p. 96) and decorate it to look like Mr McGregor's garden. Make some gingery rabbit and hedgehog biscuits using the recipe for cinnamon cookies (p. 82).

Overleaf: For a hearty adult's high tea, serve a selection of delicacies. On the rustic seat, from the left, lemon and walnut bread (p. 83), scones (p. 97), hazelnut macaroons filled with cream (p. 100) and banana gingerbread (p. 101). Below are further temptations in the shape of summer fruit sponges – here made with raspberries (p. 102) – and a coffee and hazelnut roulade (p. 60).

Opposite page 111: Garnishes (p. 129) of all kinds make a dish, I think, and you can concoct radish roses, olive rabbits, celery twirls, scored orange twirls, gherkin fans, spring onion and cucumber twirls, and vandyked tomatoes. Small individual savoury salads, such as those in the front, can garnish a starter or main course plate.

CHAPTER FIVE

DRINKS PARTIES

These vary enormously, and can range from a convivial drink with a couple of neighbours or friends, to a full-blown cocktail party with 20 or more people. I have very strong likes and dislikes as far as drinks are concerned, which you'll discover below, but I do like to make a show with some nibbles and garnishes, and you'll find some recipes and methods towards the end of the chapter.

You can hold drinks parties at home, inside or out in the garden, or anywhere you please. As one of the joys of the Lake District is, inevitably, its lakes, we literally took to the water for our drinks party on the steam launch *Kittyhawk*, from the Windermere Steamboat Museum. The latter, founded by George Pattinson, and opened in 1977 by Prince Charles, is a must for visitors to the area. It has fascinating exhibits, including Beatrix Potter's rowing boat (salvaged after 35 years at the bottom of a tarn near her house), and Dolly, the oldest propeller-driven, mechanically powered steamboat in the world (dated 1850, and confirmed by both the *Guinness Book of Records* and Lloyd's shipping records). I had already taken to the water for a party – the more mundane Orient Express steamer – for my fiftieth birthday celebrations, and it poured with rain. It is, I must admit, quite cold on Windermere a fair proportion of the year, so forewarned, I thought we'd cook up some hot toddy, great for when you've got a cold, but equally efficacious, I should think, at keeping the cold *at bay*!

Parties on the water, incidentally, are very much part of the history of Windermere. When boating became popular, so boats and the lake became fashionable, and the local Edwardian and Victorian gentry socialised on the steamers, giving afternoon tea parties. So, instead of an alcoholic drinks party, you could give a *tea* party, serving iced tea (p. 122) with some of the tea-time delights from that chapter.

For drinks parties, there are drinks and drinks, believe you me! And the governing factor is not always purely finance, for cheap drinks aren't always nasty! A good nose, eager eye and good judgement are all that are necessary on your part. (The advice of a good wine writer is vital as well, I think, and you should religiously follow their column, taking note of things that appeal to you personally.)

I seldom drink spirits, but when I have a couple of friends in, or I feel low, I love a Bloody Mary or a gin and tonic. However, both are made in a special way to meet my peculiar needs and tastes.

GIN AND TONIC

The gin has to be the Gordon's export I always buy at the duty-free – perhaps it is the attractive label that catches my eye with its juniper berries and lovely colourings. A fresh lemon half is squeezed into the generous tot of gin, lots of ice added, then half bubbling chilled tonic and half bottled spa water is poured in, with a big twist of fresh lime to finish. Crazy and very indulgent – yes, you are right, but as I only drink it occasionally I like it this way. Unfortunately, however, around the world even the famous (schhh, you know what) tonic changes in flavour. I used to think they weren't using the proper amount of quinine, but then discovered that the tonic actually depended on the kind of water used for the bottling. This came to light when the Cape Town branch of the famous company changed from well water to city water – no way could I get a G&T to my liking.

BLOODY MARY

In the States, most Bloody Marys are made from a 'Mr and Mrs T.'s Bloody Mary' mix, and when I first saw these bottles and cans I thought I would fetch them home. But, oh, they are horrible, tasting of monosodium glutamate. I use large, round cut-glass tumblers, the rims of which are dipped into egg white and then into sea salt crystals. The chilled vodka is measured in, then I add chilled tomato juice from cans, very generously seasoned with Worcestershire sauce (rather than the horribly hot Tabasco), a good shaking of celery salt, freshly ground black pepper, a celery twirl (p. 131) nicked up the middle half-way, allowing it to perch on the rim of the glass, a couple of the lovely mini cherry tomatoes (with stalks still on, making them easier for guests to eat), and a generous wedge of fresh lime, once again slit part-way between flesh and skin to allow it to sit on the opposite side from the celery. It's all garnished with a very large sprig of fresh parsley or, even better, some deep-fried parsley crushed on top.

However, with all this palaver, you couldn't feasibly serve these drinks at a larger gathering. A Pimms party would be nice in summer, and offering just that would make the service very much easier.

PIMMS

I love old-fashioned Pimms drinks, but I only like to serve them when I can get the pretty borage flowers from the herb garden (June to October here in the Lakes). I make a real MGM production number of the actual glasses: I use half-pint beer tankards, not the thick, heavy, clumsy ones, but some seconds I managed to get from Cumbria Crystal. Go to town on the fresh fruit in the glasses – apple wedges (soak these in some lime juice for half an hour and note the distinct difference), banana circles, fresh cherries, wild Alpine strawberries, thickish cucumber slices, green skin left on, orange segments, stoneless grapes, and thick circles of kiwi fruit (avoid pineapple as it is rather acidic). Be generous with your Pimms mix and then top up with fizzy, bottled lemonade. Large sprigs of fresh mint (avoid catmint) and borage complete the pretty picture, and the drink is virtually a meal in itself!

However, I always think *wine* the most sensible choice for a party of any sort, as you don't have to rush around *doing* anything, apart from pouring, of course. Always try and buy the best wines you can afford but do, as I said, follow a favourite wine writer – they're seeking out and recommending good and cheap wines as well as the out-of-reach Château Petrus! Some of my particular favourites I outline below.

In my formative days in this profession, I was introduced to Sancerre by my wonderful friend Margaret Costa. She, and only she, has the way with words that immediately conjures up the scene and setting where the grapes are grown for this wine, makes your mouth dry, anticipating the eventual drink, your nose twitch and your blood pressure rise with expectation! The colour should have a hint of crabapple green, the bouquet should be of freshly picked gooseberries and the texture should have the lightest of oils clinging to the side of the glass. So it once was, but very, very seldom now. The Sauvignon Blancs from New Zealand and Australia continue to produce an equivalent to the old-style Sancerre I was once proud to have on the wine list, and guests are constantly expressing gratified surprise when drinking these New World wines for the first time. They are 100 per cent clean and pure, with no blends, the skills of the wine-maker coming through loud and strong. The Chardonnays, too, provided you can get the older ones from 1984 or 1985, are superb, rich and buttery.

Wines in the southern hemisphere are made in February each year, so if you are only used to northern wines produced in October, remember that the southern ones are seven months older in their vintage! The problem, as far as I am concerned, is New Zealand wine-makers are unable to hold stock for long – allowing the wine to grow and develop – as they are charged duty when the wine is *made* and not (as in other countries) when it leaves their cellars. If only their Government would give them a year's grace, we would be able to enjoy their wines matured to everyone's benefit.

I also like Beaujolais wines. Brouilly and Fleurie are two of my favourites, but I always serve them chilled (they go particularly well with the main Lakeland platter of a luxurious brunch/breakfast). However, do not confuse these with Beaujolais Nouveau, which must be the biggest hype on the PR scene. All this nonsense of people rushing over to Beaune in balloons, vintage cars, helicopters in order to be the *first* to have the wine on their tables is as ridiculous as those people stupid enough to eat grouse on the 12th! A few years ago we spent a superb week's holiday cruising in a private launch on the Riviera, and were horrified to see stainless steel tanker after tanker coming ashore at Marseilles, but realised that it was October and presumably all the Algerian plonk was heading for Burgundy and eventual blending!

By no means am I an expert on wine but I do know what I like. The Spanish wines from the house of Torres have gained a lot of publicity of late, and deservedly so. At Miller Howe we sell a great deal of their Gran Viña Sol Reserva 1985, which is a superbly blended Sauvignon Blanc finished in new American oak casks, giving the wine a distinguished flavour. Their Gran Coronas 1983 is a superb robust red which goes so well with highly flavoured red meat dishes.

For parties, though, you could choose less distinguished wines. A good drink, especially in the summer, is Kir. Sweet and sickly could well be your memory of the last of these you tasted – because it was badly prepared and possibly using cheap and nasty ingredients. (Remember, nothing will disguise a bad wine – the stomach will rebel eventually and then your guests will think very badly of you.)

KIR AND KIR ROYALE

For both these a good Crème de Cassis is essential. Don't, whatever you do, attempt to use a blackcurrant essence syrup (the downfall of most Kirs, even in establishments of high repute such as Minim's of Paris). It is the percentage of Cassis used which makes a good Kir. Too little is better than too much. Simply pour out from your bottle of wine or sparkling wine 4 tablespoons of the contents and substitute with 4 tablespoons Crème de Cassis. Slowly turn the bottle upside down – cork replaced or thumb held over the top, of course – so that the syrup mixes through, resulting in a concoction resembling a light rosé wine rather than Ribena!

A Kir can be made with a dryish white wine which suits your pocket and palate, but I normally use Muscadet, Macon or Bourgogne Aligoté, in each case extremely well chilled. A Kir Royale is made from a good sparkling dry white wine.

On a hot summer's day – or in a stoked-up house on a winter's evening, for that matter – a glass of sparkling dry white wine is enhanced by a large teaspoon of elderflower sorbet. You might grimace reading about such barbaric happenings but believe you me, guests of mine have found such a mixture very refreshing. Asti Spumante, too, is a wine that wine snobs laugh about – a pity, as elderly folk love it for its sweetness. Over the festive season I put 2–3 skinned segments of tangerine on a cocktail stick in each champagne saucer glass prior to pouring on this drink.

Still on wines, for years I had an aversion to – and always declined – invitations to punch parties as I remember only too well the condition in which I woke up the next morning in my younger days. I know, alas, the true meaning of 'punch drunk' – the joy may be quick and short, but, oh, the illness slow and long! Without any doubt the worst ones were in my otherwise happy days in rep when friends (who needed enemies with this type of person around?) enthralled you with their concoctions, and invariably the thrill came from the sheer cheapness of the brew. False economy really as what was gained in the purse initially was more than lost in expenses incurred regaining normality! And I've tried the lot of the latter, from raw eggs with vinegar to arrowroot with bicarbonate of soda in tonic water with Angostura. The very worst occasion was, when working in West Africa, I stupidly consumed pints of freshly brewed palm wine mixed with pure spirit from the mine assay office. I tried to bury myself in a self-made hole under a frangipani tree. Talk about hallucinations ...

It is usually assumed these days that punch is served hot, but that need not necessarily be the case, and I give below a few ideas for chilled wine punches. Fashionable folk go the whole hog, and spend an arm and a leg on silver or cut-glass punch bowls with la-di-dah ladles. I settle for a large Pyrex bowl which has endless uses in the kitchen, and an ordinary stainless steel sauce ladle. I am fortunate in having some lovely Cumbria Crystal chunky tumblers, but Woolworth's Jacobean are just as practical!

Depending on what takes your fancy, pipped grapes, a $\frac{1}{2}$ teaspoon of Granadilla, sultanas or raisins left overnight to plump up in cooking brandy, pomegranate pips with jelly, red, black or white currants in summer, thin apple wedges or orange segments can all be used as garnishes, as well as many fresh herbs! Initially follow the ideas to the letter, always use wine that you yourself would drink by the glass with food, and then experiment yourself, taking out items which spoil your pleasure, and adding extras to suit your personal palate.

Hot Sweet Rosé Punch

· *serves 6–8* ·

1 bottle rosé wine
4 oz (100 g) caster sugar
rind of 1 orange and 1 lemon
4 cloves
1 whole nutmeg, finely grated
$\frac{1}{2}$ cinnamon stick

Pour all the ingredients into a saucepan and bring to the boil. Pass through a sieve and serve at once.

SIMPLE HOT PUNCH

——— · • · ———

· *serves 8* ·

1 pint (600 ml) lager
1 pint (600 ml) cider of choice
a pinch each of ground cloves, ginger, and allspice
$\frac{1}{2}$ cinnamon stick
5 fl oz (150 ml) brandy
2 tablespoons soft brown sugar

for the garnish
orange wedges
apple circles

Put all the ingredients except the brandy and sugar into a saucepan and bring to the boil. Remove, and stir in the brandy and sugar, stirring until the latter is dissolved. Serve with orange wedges and apple circles.

HOT RED WINE PUNCH

——— · • · ———

· *serves 6–8* ·

1 bottle Cabernet Sauvignon
5 fl oz (150 ml) pure apple juice
3 tablespoons runny honey
$\frac{1}{2}$ cinnamon stick
8 cloves

Put all the ingredients into a saucepan and bring to the boil. Pass through a sieve and serve at once.

CHILLED CHAMPAGNE STRAWBERRY CUPS

———— · • · ————

· *serves 8* ·

juice and finely grated rind of 1 orange
8 fresh strawberries, mashed then rubbed through a fine
plastic sieve
1 bottle cheap champagne (or sparkling white wine), well
chilled
$\frac{1}{2}$ bottle dry white wine, well chilled

for the garnish
mint sprigs or cherries

Divide the rind and juice of the orange and the strawberry purée
between 8 glasses. Divide out the sparkling white wine and dry white
wine similarly. Garnish with sprigs of mint or, in summer, cherries
joined by their stalk (one in the glass, one hanging outside).

SWEET SUMMER SPARKLE

———— · • · ————

· *serves 6–8* ·

ice cubes
summer fruits (as for Pimms, p. 115)
$\frac{1}{2}$ bottle sweet dessert wine, well chilled
$1\frac{1}{2}$ pints (900 ml) lemonade, well chilled

for the garnish
twists and twirls of lemon rind (p. 130) or egg white and
coloured caster sugar

Divide the ice cubes between 6–8 glasses, and put some fresh
summer fruits in each. Combine the dessert wine and lemonade, and
pour into the glasses. Serve immediately, garnishing with the twists
and twirls of lemon rind, or take a little trouble beforehand and make
the glasses look nice: put the white of an egg on a saucer, dip the rims
of the glasses in this and immediately into coloured caster sugar.

Watermelon Punch

—— ·•· ——

This is an unusual, but simple, punch, which is aimed at teetotallers mainly – as the watermelon flesh really takes over, so even they will be fooled! (But if they've truly signed the pledge, use half lemonade and half soda water, adding a few spots of Angostura Bitters.)

· serves about 15 ·

1 small watermelon
3 bottles sparkling or dry white wine, well chilled
crushed ice

for the garnish
mint leaves

Wipe the outside of the watermelon with a damp cloth and straighten off one end so that it stands up like a rugby football waiting for a try to be scored. With a felt pen draw a handle and the outline of a basket two-thirds of the way up the side and using a very sharp, small, serrated knife cut out the basket. Remove all the flesh from the base and top, discard the seeds, then liquidise all the flesh and pass through a plastic sieve. Combine flesh with the sparkling or white wine, and put as much as you can into the basket at the last moment. Serve cold in glasses with crushed ice, and garnish with mint leaves.

These punches, whether hot or cold, are all delightful but, if a punch means a mixed drink of sorts, then my favourite winter 'punches' are still those made to take up to bed, or better still, to take on a long train journey in a flask (makes the other passengers look like the original, anticipatory Bisto Kids!). There are a few following the iced tea which are still a little alcoholic, but all medicinal of course . . .

ICED TEA

Coming from the north of England I am forever 'brewing up' and can well remember my grandmother having a hideous, large, brown glazed teapot forever on the go in her kitchen, so it is difficult, in some ways, to realise tea has only been part of British cuisine and tradition for the last 130 odd years.

I like to use crystal whisky tumblers for this drink as, arranged on silver tray, they reflect the ingredients beautifully and are a conversation piece to start off any occasion. Thin slices of scored lemon – pips removed – are put in along with an assortment of freshly picked rose petals and a couple of sprigs of mint (have to hand a borage sprig for the final garnish). Make the tea in the normal way using the tea you like and which suits your water (often a tricky task these days with local water varying in chlorine content). Put 3–4 ice cubes into each glass and strain the hot tea on after it has brewed for 3–4 minutes. At the farm my current favourite in a pint (600 ml) teapot is a brew of 2 Indian tea bags plus a heaped teaspoon of Earl Grey, but I love all sorts of teas and nearly always can come up with at least a dozen to tempt my weary palate. In the summer, mango or blackcurrant teas are delicious, but if you do decide to buy one of these for the first time, buy the smallest amount possible to make sure it is to your personal taste.

CURRIED BEEF TEA

———— ·•· ————

This is ideal to welcome guests back from a brisk morning walk and, minus the cream topping, it is good to take in a flask for a hike!

· serves 4–6 ·

1 × 15 oz (425 g) can consommé (*not* condensed)
5 fl oz (150 ml) sherry
$\frac{1}{4}$ teaspoon curry powder of choice

for the garnish
double cream, whipped
4–6 cheese croûton triangles (p. 71)

Mix the ingredients together, heat through, then pour into glasses. Hold a teaspoon over, then float some double cream over the spoon bowl (as for Irish coffee) on top. Serve with cheese croûton triangles.

SHERRY FLIP

———— ·•· ————

On a winter's day here's a daredevil drink for elevenses which will lighten the heart – and head – and which has tremendous medicinal benefits. Well, I think so . . .

· per person ·

5 fl oz (150 ml) sherry
1 egg
1 teaspoon soft brown sugar
1 tablespoon single or whipping cream

for the garnish
freshly grated nutmeg

Liquidise or beat all the ingredients together and then bring up to a warm temperature. Don't let it get too hot. Serve immediately, topped with the merest touch of freshly grated nutmeg.

BOBBY'S HOT TODDY

As I said earlier, this is remarkable for when you feel a cold coming on. Take it just before retiring.

· per sick person ·

a generous measure of malt whisky
juice of $\frac{1}{2}$ fresh lemon
$\frac{1}{2}$ teaspoon caster sugar
$\frac{1}{2}$ teaspoon runny honey

Warm through the glass, then add the whisky, lemon juice, sugar and honey. Stir well and, after putting a silver teaspoon in the glass, pour in 3 measures of boiling water. Sip at once.

INDULGENT INVALID NIGHTCAPS

· per person ·

1 mug or beaker fresh milk
plus
1 teaspoon instant coffee with 1 tablespoon brandy
or
2 teaspoons drinking chocolate with 1 tablespoon dark rum
or
1 teaspoon cocoa powder with 1 tablespoon dark rum
and
1–2 teaspoons soft brown sugar or honey
an extremely generous scattering of freshly grated nutmeg

Simply put all the ingredients into a saucepan and whisk together until the milk begins to boil. Pour into the warmed mug or beaker.

The coffee-based drink is enhanced by the merest touch of freshly grated lemon rind; the cocoa or drinking chocolate with the merest touch of freshly grated orange rind. And, to be really sluttish, the latter can have a bit of a Cadbury's flake broken on the top!

So now I've described all the drinks *I* like, and out of which selection I'm sure you can find something to suit any occasion (even that potentially sad duo going off to bed with incipient flu!), I'll get to the food for drinks parties.

SAVOURY CROISSANTS

This cream cheese pastry is delicious and light, but don't try to make it in the height of summer – it needs to be cool and well chilled at all times.

You can fill the croissants with anything you like: a good filling consists of a 9 oz (250 g) can of sardines mashed with 2 hard-boiled eggs, parsley and a little curry powder. Or you can use one of those given for the puff pastry rounds on p. 72. A smoked haddock and cheesey filling would be good too, and in each case, you need about 8–9 oz (225–250 g) filling.

· *makes 20–24 croissants* ·

6 oz (175 g) soft butter
6 oz (175 g) good cream cheese
8 oz (225 g) plain flour, sieved
filling of choice (see above)

Put the soft butter, cheese and flour into the mixer bowl and mix to a dough, or cream the butter and cheese together by hand, then fold in the sieved flour. Leave to chill for 2 hours. Meanwhile prepare the filling.

Roll the dough out very thinly on a lightly floured work surface. Cut in to 5 in (13 cm) squares and then halve each square to make a triangle. Put a teaspoon of the chosen filling into the centre of each triangle and then roll from the long edge towards the point to enclose the filling. Curl round to make a croissant shape.

Place on a baking tray and leave to chill for a further 2 hours. Pre-heat the oven to gas mark 7, 425°F (220°C), and bake for 20 minutes. Nicest served warm.

TAPENADE WITH GARLIC SOLDIERS

——— · · ———

I can think of nothing better to eat on a day in summer when pre-meal drinks can be imbibed out of doors, as it recaptures happy times in Provence. The dip is better if it is made the day before and left overnight, covered with cling film, in the fridge.

· *serves 6–8* ·

tapenade
25 stoned black olives
10 anchovy fillets
4 heaped tablespoons canned drained tuna
2 tablespoons capers
5 fl oz (150 ml) good olive oil

garlic soldiers
6 bread slices, crusts removed
6 oz (175 g) garlic butter (p. 153), melted

Make the *tapenade* first. Place all the ingredients except for the oil in a food processor, and begin to blend on high speed. Very slowly, dribble in the oil, and when it has been absorbed, it is ready. Remove to a bowl, cover with cling film and chill.

The next day, make the garlic soldiers. Pre-heat the oven to gas mark 4, 350°F (180°C), and cut each bread slice into 4–5 strips. Coat with the melted garlic butter, then place on a baking tray. Bake in the pre-heated oven for 10 minutes then turn over and bake for up to 5 minutes more. They should be golden and crisp. Remove and leave to drain and dry on a double thickness of kitchen paper.

I usually serve the *tapenade* in a cut-glass Regency wine-glass cooler that has been painted inside with walnut oil and then sprinkled with 3–4 tablespoons finely chopped herbs. Put the herbs into the greased bowl, then turn the dish on its side and roll the herbs around in a tumbling fashion so that they coat the base and sides. Then pour or spoon in your 'dip', and let people use the rich buttery croûtons to scoop it up. (You could, of course, if it's not too runny, *spread* the *tapenade* on the croûtons.)

CROÛTON-BASED CANAPÉS

These are made like the garlic soldiers above. A slice of bought bread will give you 4 rounds (cut with an appropriately sized circular cutter), and you dip these into melted butter – plain or flavoured – and bake as above.

They can be topped with a piped outer circle of cheese and herb pâté (p. 38), and then with a $\frac{1}{2}$ teaspoon of your favourite chutney in the middle and a small sprig of parsley. (We served a very similar croûton along with the baked avocado on p. 94.) Your own home-made pâté, or some left-over meats simply blended in the food processor with a little mustard, tomato paste or creamed horseradish to bind, can be used as a topping as well. It isn't a case of you being mean using up left-overs – you are simply inventing combinations to tempt the palate.

DEEP-FRIED CURRIED LEEK RINGS

These make delicious snacks at a drinks party, but are a little greasy despite thorough draining – so have plenty of paper napkins available. The rings are also good on *top* of things – croûtons spread with something delicious like cheese and herb pâté (p. 38), or soups as a garnish.

Simply top and tail and remove the outer leaves of as many large leeks as you like, then slice them fairly finely at an angle to get a bigger ring. Put into a bowl or sink full of cold water and break up the circle slices into individual rings. Strain to remove surplus water, then leave to drain thoroughly on kitchen paper.

Put into a bowl of cold milk (use this afterwards in a sauce or similar), and then into a sieve to strain off excess. Coat with lightly curried seasoned flour – a rough guide is 1 teaspoon curry powder to 4 tablespoons plain flour, but you can experiment.

Pre-heat a deep fryer or a pan of good vegetable oil to 360°F (182°C). Shake the leek rings to get rid of surplus flour, then deep-fry them for $1\frac{1}{2}$ minutes until brown in batches. Drain well on kitchen paper and try to serve hot.

CHEDDAR CHEESE PASTRY TARTLETS

—— ·•· ——

This pastry is an old favourite of mine, which will make mini tartlets for canapés, quiches, or it's ideal for an apple pie. There's an old Lancashire (or is it Yorkshire?) saying that an apple pie without the cheese is like a kiss without a squeeze!

It's a soft pastry, and needs to be well chilled before you start to work it, but it's easy to make.

· makes about 30 × 3 in (7.5 cm) tartlets ·

10 oz (275 g) plain flour, sieved
a pinch of salt
10 oz (275 g) soft butter
10 oz (275 g) mature Cheddar cheese, finely grated

Sieve the flour and salt into your mixing bowl, and then rub in the soft butter, followed by the grated cheese. Chill well before rolling: see the quiche recipe pastry for more detailed instructions (p. 34).

Roll, cut out – into 3 in (7.5 cm) circles, or larger if you like (depending on the type and size of patty/bun tins you have) – chill, then blind-bake as for quiches, at gas mark 3, 325°F (160°C) for about 15–20 minutes, then cool. Cook for 5–10 minutes longer if this is to be the tartlet's *final* baking.

For the fillings, you can come up with quite a few, I'm sure. If you bake the tartlets off completely, so that they are ready to eat, you could leave them to cool, then pipe in a twirl of cheese and herb pâté (p. 38), avocado mousse or purée (pp. 140 and 93); you could also fold some poached salmon or prawns into some mayonnaise. For hot tartlets, you could pour some of the quiche custard on p. 36 into the blind-baked cases and bake off with a variety of added ingredients; some of the fillings for the puff pastry rounds (p. 72) could be adapted and used; and indeed many of the ramekin-baked mousses or savoury creams could be transposed into and baked in the tartlets (see pp. 16, 17 and 149).

DATES STUFFED WITH STEAMED GARLIC

These are very nice served as part of a display of canapés pre dinner, or at a drinks party, and are very easy to do. Using steamed garlic cloves as on p. 153, all you do is skin fresh dates, remove the stones and where the stone was, insert a steamed garlic clove. Serve on a cocktail stick.

Another way of using these is to thread 2–3 on a cocktail stick and serve with roast duck or pork, or the barbecue-coated chicken on p. 49.

Fresh dates are a seasonal fruit, but more and more I am finding I can buy them all year round, having been frozen over here by importers. There is very little difference, apart from the skins being more difficult to peel. For another, sweet, date idea, see p. 166.

GARNISHES

On the day you are entertaining, if you are anything like me, there is a moment when the kitchen looks like a battlefield: there is no sign of the sink, all the cupboard doors seem to be open – drawers too – your utensil/gadget holder is devoid of everything, your feet are aching (your head too, possibly), and you are getting slightly uptight. Watch out for these danger signs, and immediately take action. First of all put the kettle on, those of you who find a cuppa will do the trick, but most sensible sinful cooks will just go to the drinks cupboard and mix a stiff one. A large initial gulp, and then it's roll up the sleeves and tackle the debris. Having done this (and, surprisingly enough, it doesn't take all that long), a semblance of order and sanity is restored.

To make sure it lasts, however, pour another drink and then play about with the garnishings. They are not costly money wise, but are time-consuming; they're also peace-inducing, and make all the difference to one's presentation of dishes. I would, just occasionally, like to be a fly on the roof of certain guests' cars after they have had dinner with me. Safely out of eye and earshot, one may be heard to say, 'Did you see all that razzmatazz with the custard starter [quiche]?' I would immediately fly up their nose for having got up mine, and annoy them all the way home! Entertaining should *be* entertainment, and it is all the radish flowers and celery twirls that garnish the dishes that make it a 'right grand do' as they say in Lancashire.

The beauty of garnishes such as those following is that, in the morning, they can be arranged on white, lipped plastic trays and, covered with generous cling film, they will come to no harm in the fridge or a cool place. You must be very generous with the cling film, however, to make sure it not only covers all the food *on* the tray, but goes underneath adequately all round to protect the food completely from the elements.

CITRUS FRUIT

Segments of lemon, lime, orange or grapefruit (p. 10) make good garnishes, as do wedges or slices of the whole fruit. Make the rinds look more interesting by scoring them with a scorer in even lines around, top to bottom; never waste the 'scorings', but blanch them and use in a garnishing capacity as well, in savoury salads, or tied in a knot on top of a shortbread tartlet perhaps (p. 162). A scored fruit can be cut into twirls: cut half-way through the fruit from stalk end to the opposite end, then slice as normal and twist each cut slice into a twirl.

CUCUMBER TWIRLS

These too can be scored lengthwise then sliced and cut half-way through the circumference for a twirl. (See p. 110.)

GHERKIN FANS

Place a small, sweet pickled gherkin on your cutting board. Using a small, very sharp knife, cut along the length of the gherkin about 5 times, keeping it all joined at one end. Fan the slices out with your fingers. (See p. 110.)

OLIVE RABBITS

Take a large firm olive with the stone in. Cut off a small oval lengthwise slice for it to sit firmly on. Cut a small V from one end of this slice for the rabbit's ears and slot the slice into a nick at one end of the olive body. (See p. 110.)

TOMATOES

Halved tomatoes can be cleaned of flesh and seeds, and used as a colourful container for something. You could also cut a tomato almost through towards the top, so that you have a *lid*, then clean out the seeds and flesh. Filled with cheese and herb pâté and topped with a sprig of parsley, it would be nice on a cheeseboard. Cut a tomato into vandyked halves by zig-zagging all round instead of cutting in a straight line (see p. 110). You could make a tomato basket, cutting round, but leaving a 'handle'.

SPRING ONION TWIRLS

Top and tail spring onions, trim away the outer skin, then make as many little cuts as you are able into and along the green stalk length of the onion, leaving the white bulb intact. Leave to soak in iced water and the cut stems will blossom out. (See p. 110.)

CELERY TWIRLS

Cut washed celery sticks into 2 in (5 cm) strips. Using a very sharp small knife, make lots of little cuts in down the lengthwise grain of the strips. Do this at the top and bottom, leaving a bit uncut in the middle to hold the 'fringes' together. Now cut *through* these little cuts, dividing the fringed ends, top and bottom, in half. Leave in iced water and the fringes or tassels will curl out beautifully. (See p. 110.)

RADISH FLOWERS

Wash, top and tail some radishes. Place on their stalk ends, cutting off a tiny slice if they don't sit properly. Cut out a little V section across the top of the radish – it looks like 'lips'. Do this again at right angles to the first cut, then again twice diagonally so that you have a 'Union Jack' star on the top. Make about 8 tiny curving slicing cuts into the radish towards the base going about two-thirds of the way down. Don't cut *through*. The cuts will open up into flowers after a soaking of about 4–5 hours in iced water, and the top star looks particularly pretty (see p. 110). These are also nice served as a canapé, to dip into a dish of coarse sea salt.

OTHER GARNISHES

Think about the decorative possibilities of halved pipped grapes, quartered strawberries with their green stalks left on (much more colourful and visual), and skinned fresh dates.

SAVOURY SALADS

The tempting savoury salads (p. 110) are also assembled in the morning like the other garnishes, and then all you require at the last minute is a palette knife to convey them from tray to serving plate.... So, you leave the dining room, are away 4 minutes or so, and return with 6 plates of quiche garnished with a lovely fresh salad. Guests will be full of admiration and wonder – but don't tell them the secret, suggest they buy this book!

Have ready in front of you a small plastic tray with a side lip on which to arrange your salads. Per salad, you need a lettuce leaf of about 3–4 in (8–10 cm) in diameter, plus a smaller radiccio leaf for colour if you like to place on top. Pipe a twirl of whipped cream or cheese and herb pâté (p. 38) into the middle of the leaf to act as an anchor. Into this arrange a variety of garnishes from above, not forgetting about half walnuts, herb flowers, red pepper or onion circles (don't let these overpower the salad or the dish the salad is to accompany), drained canned red kidney beans etc. Chill until needed, but allow to come back to room temperature before serving.

PIPING

Using a piping bag in a professional manner will add a flourish and flair to your entertaining. Buy medium plastic piping bags and always use *plastic* star and plain piping nozzles. (Tin ones are available, but I have seen too many septic cuts from these after hands are plunged into the washing-up water.)

Practise at first by using dehydrated potato whipped up to the consistency of whipped cream. As you empty the bag on your efforts just scoop up what you have piped out, put it back in the bag and carry on practising. Then throw it out!

When first starting to use a piping bag the thing that everybody does wrong straightaway is to put far too much filling in. First put your star nozzle in the end of the bag, then put the bag into a large jug or vase. The bag can stand upright with the top 2 in (5 cm) of the open end hanging down over the outside. In other words the vase or jug fully supports the bag leaving both your hands free to put the cream in! Do so, filling about two-thirds only. Bring the overlapping top end of the bag up in one hand and remove the full bag from the container with the other hand, the thumb and index finger open wide and grabbing the neck. Start to force the contents down to the bottom of the bag and as soon as you see some appearing from the nozzle, *stop*. Twist the empty top round to maintain pressure on the contents of the bag.

Your work hand – thumb and index finger – should be comfortable and able to glide to and fro, and the other three fingers should be exerting pressure on the full bag to allow the contents to come out readily and easily (rather like playing the bagpipes). Individual stars are 'dropped off'; the edges of gâteaux are decorated by using a small continuous circular movement; and a fancy 'big dipper' outside edge is obtained by forcing down on the surface with the bag going slightly away from you then easing the pressure while you bring the bag *up* towards you. It's difficult to describe in words, but get your potato, and practise until perfect!

CHAPTER SIX

DINNER PARTIES

When giving a *grand* party in every sense of the word – best china, cutlery, cruet sets, candelabra with big candles that you will light (one of my pet hates is *un*lit candles in a candelabra or a flower arrangement) – you must obviously be organised as far as food, drinks, service etc are concerned. You will have plotted a balanced and sensible menu; worked out the logistics of hot dishes and oven space; and ensured that at least one-half of the dishes can be pre-prepared so that you've only a limited amount of work on the night itself.

You will have worked out the wines to accompany the food, and will have the requisite number of whites chilling in the fridge, and reds coming to room temperature. The glasses should be given a final polish in the late afternoon when they are placed on the table. Try to lay your table earlier on in the day too, for this is one more job out of the way, and in fact, with that done to your satisfaction – I *love* laying tables splendidly – you'll feel you're almost there. Don't worry if your dinner service is for six and you've asked eight for a meal; give the hosts the two odd plates. In fact, the more variety of plates the better, I think, and I'm continually scouring junk shops and buying. If you're catering for even larger numbers – for a really grand party of 50, say – there are many places where you can hire plates and cutlery (they sometimes even take them back dirty).

As for the service of the food, I always think it's best – whether you're catering for 8 or 50 – to arrange the food on the plate in the kitchen to be put directly in front of the guests. None of those vegetable tureens for me that are passed around the table like long-lost souls. With all that to-ing and fro-ing, there is no way that food can reach everybody's plate nice and hot. In fact, make sure you urge guests – especially at a large party – to tuck in rather than wait. The food should cover the whole centre part of the plate and look attractive (add some of those garnishes you made earlier on in the day), for enjoyment of food is almost as much to do with what it *looks* like as what it *tastes* like. (In fact, I'll never understand why china makers go so much for centred patterns on plates: only the *rims* are seen when the plates are full.)

Some time on a dinner party day (just after you have done all the garnishes, perhaps), go through the meal course by course, and visualise not only how and what you are going to serve, but how you are going to stage-manage the event. Obviously you want the kitchen cooking and serving arrangements to go smoothly, but you have also got to consider where to put everything as the dirty dishes start coming back, course by course. I have seen hostesses looking radiant at the beginning of a meal and fully in control, to find smiles sagging more and more: if there's no organisation in the kitchen, the clutter can build up very quickly indeed. *Everything* that goes into the dining room has to come back and has either to be stacked, put into the dishwasher or actually washed in the sink! Don't clutter up every inch of work space with foodstuffs and courses but remember to have a corner (preferably close to the sink) where you can systematically stack the dirties. Save gallon cream and ice-cream containers as they are marvellous, half filled with boiling water and a touch of detergent, for putting all the dirty cutlery into (handles outward to the top). If you have time, you could at least rinse all the dirty plates before stacking them (this helps with the next day's task of washing up).

I love giving dinner parties – in one sense, I suppose I could be said to give a dinner party every night of the week at Miller Howe – but to hold a grand dinner somewhere like Belle Isle would be a truly splendid occasion. This unique circular Georgian house stands on an island in the middle of Lake Windermere (you can only get to it by boat), and has belonged to the Curwen family since 1781. It used to be open to the public, but now, because of Susan Curwen's determination to keep the house (her husband died a few years ago), the house and the 40-acre island are being turned into a conference centre, with outstanding facilities. It would be an ideal and wonderfully romantic setting for a wedding reception or richly celebratory dinner.

MENU ONE

SAVARIN OF SOLE STUFFED WITH PRAWNS *148*

CHESTNUT-STUFFED FILLET STEAK WRAPPED IN BACON *152*

CHOCOLATE SHORTBREAD TARTLETS WITH
CHOCOLATE ORANGE CREAM *162*

———·•·———

MENU TWO

AVOCADO MOUSSE GÂTEAU WITH CHEESE AND
HERB PÂTÉ ON CURRIED BISCUIT BASE *140*

SAVOURY SOLE FILLET BAKED WITH MAYONNAISE *147*

PEARS POACHED IN CIDER *165*

———·•·———

MENU THREE

TRIO OF SALMON *142*

BONED STUFFED LEG OF LAMB *155*

FRUIT PURÉES *161*

———·•·———

AVOCADO MOUSSE GÂTEAU WITH CHEESE AND HERB PÂTÉ ON CURRIED BISCUIT BASE

——— ·•· ———

Its title may be a mouthful, to say the least, but what a delicious mouthful it proves to be when you serve it! I even put a spooonful of aïoli (p. 57) alongside to make the tastebuds work even harder! It is becoming one of the most popular new dishes at Miller Howe.

· *makes a 10 in (25 cm) gâteau* ·

for the base and sides
10 oz (275 g) digestive biscuits
2 level tablespoons curry powder
2 oz (50 g) butter, melted
10 oz (275 g) cheese and herb pâté (p. 38)

avocado mousse
½ oz (15 g) powdered gelatine
8 tablespoons white wine
6 ripe avocado pears
10 fl oz (300 ml) home-made mayonnaise (p. 56)
5 fl oz (150 ml) double cream, lightly whipped
1 teaspoon salt

for the garnish
8 oz (225 g) tomatoes, skinned, seeded and finely chopped
toasted sesame seeds (p. 11)

Pre-heat the oven to gas mark 4, 350°F (180°C) and line a 10 in (25 cm) loose-bottomed, spring-sided cake tin with good greaseproof paper.

For the base, break the biscuits into pieces and work to crumbs in your liquidiser, along with the curry powder. Fold in the melted butter and spread this dough across the base of the lined tin. Bake in the pre-heated oven for 15 minutes, and then allow to go cold before doing anything else.

When cold, pipe the cheese and herb pâté around the sides and up towards the top edge of the tin.

For the mousse, put the gelatine in a small pan and pour in the white wine all in one go. Leave to one side (p. 79).

Peel and quarter the avocados and mix to a smooth paste in your blender. Blend in the mayonnaise, whipped cream and salt. Reconstitute the gelatine (p. 79) by heating very gently until the liquid is clear, and then passing through a warmed metal sieve. Fold well into the mixture. Pour this into the centre of the lined cake tin and chill to set, about 4 hours.

Take the sides off the tin and garnish the top of the gâteau with the 'concasse' tomatoes and sesame seeds. It will slice easily if you use a sharp knife dunked into a jug of very hot water after every slice.

CUCUMBER CREAMS

These interesting little gelatine-set creams can be served as a starter at a lunch or dinner (or indeed a picnic).

· *serves 6* ·

$\frac{1}{4}$ cucumber, wiped and halved
$\frac{1}{2}$ oz (15 g) powdered gelatine
5 tablespoons white wine
5 fl oz (150 ml) double cream
a pinch of salt
1 teaspoon caster sugar
1 tablespoon white wine vinegar
6 oz (175 g) cream cheese
2 egg whites, stiffly beaten
curry powder (optional)

Remove the seeds and watery flesh of the cucumber halves, then chop the flesh very finely – leaving the skin *on*. Put the gelatine in a small pan and pour in the white wine all in one go. Leave to one side (see p. 79).

Lightly beat the cream with the salt and sugar, and carefully beat in the wine vinegar. Combine this with the cream cheese, then fold in the cucumber. Taste and adjust the seasoning if necessary.

Reconstitute the gelatine by putting on the lowest heat possible until clear, then pouring through a warmed metal sieve (p. 79). Fold in well, and then fold in the stiffly beaten egg whites. Grease 6 ramekins and sprinkle the bases and sides with a little curry powder if wished. Divide the cream mixture among the ramekins. Leave to chill and set, about 2 hours. Either turn out to serve, or eat from the ramekin.

TRIO OF SALMON

This consists of slices of smoked salmon, *gravadlax* (marinated salmon), and poached fresh salmon, and invariably provokes much comment and talk at the table. The individual plates can be assembled a couple of hours before your guests arrive and covered with cling film.

· serves 6 ·

12 oz (350 g) each of fresh salmon, smoked salmon and
gravadlax (p. 45)
white wine
olive oil

for the garnish
hard-boiled egg slices, radish flowers, cherry tomatoes,
lemon wedges or twirls, fresh dill

If you cut *all* the salmon types wafer thin with your serrated knife – as you would smoked salmon – each portion will look far more generous. Allow each plate about 2 oz (50 g) of each type of fish.

Poach the fresh salmon 'escalopes' in a baking tray on your hob. Cover the bottom with a mixture of half water and white wine and a tablespoon of olive oil, bring to the boil, and place the salmon escalopes in. Simmer for 2–3 minutes only. Drain and leave to cool.

Arrange the three types of salmon artistically on individual plates, and garnish similarly. In the middle of the plate you could have a slice of hard-boiled egg topped with a radish flower and, if you can find them, 3 cherry tomatoes separating the salmons look very nice. Finish off with a wedge or twirl of lemon and couple of sprigs of dill.

Opposite: A trio of salmon (above) makes a splendidly luxurious starter for a dinner – a couple of slices each of poached fresh, marinated (gravadlax) and smoked. A trio of fruit purées (p. 161) – apple and lime on the bottom, mango in the middle and pineapple on the top – makes for an equally fine pudding.

Overleaf: A selection of drinks to serve at a drinks party or before dinner (pp. 114–124) – including Kir and an iced tea (for teetotallers?), with some substantial nibbles: cheese pastry tartlets (p. 128) filled with avocado mousse (p. 140) and cheese and herb pâté (p. 38), stuffed dates (p. 129), savoury croissants (p. 125) and tapenade with garlic soldiers (p. 126).

Savoury Sole Fillet Baked with Mayonnaise

————— · • · —————

This is a quick version of what tastes like the traditional sole with tartare sauce, once on every grand station-hotel menu in days of old. When I got the idea, my immediate reaction was that the mayonnaise would split while cooking; on the contrary, it seems to blend with the fleshy fish, to make a deliciously tasty dish.

One major advantage is that the fish can be pre-prepared in the morning and left, covered with cling film, until you want to cook it.

· *serves 6 as a starter, 3 for a main course* ·

6 fillets of sole
10 fl oz (300 ml) home-made mayonnaise (p. 57)

savoury breadcrumbs
8 oz (225 g) very fine breadcrumbs
2 oz (50 g) onion, very finely chopped
1 oz (25 g) strong Cheddar cheese, finely grated
1 garlic clove, peeled and crushed to a paste with salt
2 tablespoons finely chopped parsley

Make the savoury breadcrumbs first. Either put everything into a processor or blender and chop and mix finely; or do everything by hand, making sure the onion, garlic and parsley are very *finely* chopped. Mix together well. (Store any left-overs in a screw-top jar in the fridge.)

Pre-heat the oven to gas mark 4, 350°F (180°C), and bone and skin the sole. Wipe dry on kitchen paper or cloth.

Place the mayonnaise in one of those large, old-fashioned soup dishes and the breadcrumbs in another. Slip-slop each fillet first into the mayonnaise, coating both sides, then into the breadcrumbs, making sure they are coated thoroughly.

Transfer to a baking tray and bake in the pre-heated oven for 20 minutes. Serve a starter portion with a little savoury salad (p. 132), or a main course with some vegetables.

Opposite: For a magnificent dinner, serve a chestnut-stuffed fillet steak garnished with steamed garlic (pp. 152–3) and a selection of vegetables, to be followed by chocolate shortbread tartlets (p. 162) filled with orange mousse (p. 164).

SAVARIN OF SOLE STUFFED WITH PRAWNS

——— ·•· ———

This dish can be prepared the day before without coming to any harm, and it looks nice for a buffet party with a dessertspoon of home-made mayonnaise coating it at the last moment. The fish does shrink a little when being cooked in the ramekin but have faith, when it's taken out and filled, it retains its shape.

· per person ·

melted butter
salt and freshly ground black pepper
1 boned, skinned fillet of sole, weighing approx. 4 oz (100 g)
1 tablespoon dry white wine
1 tablespoon good cream cheese
1 tablespoon double cream
8 prawns

for the garnish
1 dessertspoon home-made mayonnaise (p. 57)
a parsley sprig

Paint the base and sides of a 3 in (7.5 cm) ramekin liberally with butter and then season with salt and pepper. Wrap the fillet of sole round the outer edge and overlap the ends – vital so the fish will eventually stick together. Put the white wine into the middle of each sole-lined ramekin, cover the whole with cling film, and leave in the fridge for about 4 hours.

Pre-heat the oven to gas mark 4, 350°F (180° C), and put hard balls of crumpled greaseproof paper into the centre of each ramekin to fill it: this helps support the fish walls. Put the ramekins into a bain-marie, place in the oven and cook for 20 minutes. Leave to go cold.

When you wish to serve, beat together the cream cheese and cream and fold in the prawns. Turn the sole 'lining' out of the ramekin on to a serving plate with the side that was uppermost in the ramekin to the foot now. Spoon the cream filling into the sole circle, and garnish with the mayonnaise and parsley.

RICH SMOKED HADDOCK AND CHEESE SAVOURIES

——— · • · ———

These make a delightful starter to a dinner party, and all the preparation can be done earlier in the day. Serve with finger strips of warm toast or the wholemeal bread on p. 84. Rich and nurseryish, to be eaten with a teaspoon out of the ramekin.

· serves 6 ·

15 fl oz (450 ml) double cream
a pinch of salt
6 oz (175 g) strong Cheddar cheese, finely grated
12 oz (350 g) smoked haddock, boned, skinned and flaked

for the garnish
6 large sprigs fresh parsley

Put the double cream into a deep pan with the salt, and bubble gently, half on, half off the element or flames, for about 20–30 minutes until reduced by half. It's important to keep the heat *low*. There's no need to stir.

Pre-heat the oven to gas mark 4, 350°F (180°C), and prepare a roasting tray for use as a bain-marie.

Mix the grated cheese with the smoked haddock flakes and divide between 6 × 3 in (7.5 cm) ramekins. Pour on the reduced cream and place the ramekins in a little hot water in the bain-marie. Place in the pre-heated oven and bake for 15 minutes. Garnish with the parsley.

SMOKED SALMON, SOLE AND ASPARAGUS CREAMS

——— · • · ———

These little hot mousses never fail to produce gasps of admiration from diners and they do look rather splendid as well as tasting divine. They are also very easy to make. They're not cheap, though, so you won't churn them out daily for the family, but will save them for special occasions. However, you should really have a trial run on the family *first*, and follow the instructions implicitly: no cheating, cutting down on ingredients or taking shortcuts please, as I want you to have the satisfaction of getting a nigh perfect result first time round.

Miller Howe is often asked to cook dinners in other venues and more often than not I make certain that a fish cream similar to this is on the menu as the uninitiated are in awe of the dish. In all the years of doing these, I've only had one disaster (and even then the guests loved it): in Washington they gave us long-life heavy (double) cream, not fresh, so there was little body to the dish at the end.

A food processor is essential, but half the ingredients can be prepared in a liquidiser. Serve with a warm blender hollandaise (p. 159), flavoured appropriately if you like.

· serves 6 ·

a little melted butter
salt and freshly ground black pepper
6 strips smoked salmon, roughly 8 × 2 in (20 × 5 cm), to line
the sides and bottom outside edge of 6 ramekins
12 oz (350 g) fresh sole, skinned and boned, cut into pieces
a pinch each of cayenne pepper and freshly grated nutmeg
3 eggs
just over 10 fl oz (300 ml) double cream
6 asparagus tips, washed

to serve
blender hollandaise (p. 159)
Keta (American red salmon caviar roe)
fresh dill

Rub the melted butter over the base and up the sides of the 6 ramekins, then season with a little salt, more generously with pepper. Line the sides of the ramekins (allowing a little to rest on the base edge) with the smoked salmon, and place on a baking tray with a side lip. Cover with cling film.

Put the pieces of sole into the food processor with some salt, the cayenne and nutmeg, and turn on to high speed. One at a time add the eggs. Before adding the final one, turn off the machine, remove the lid, and with a spatula wipe down the sides, making sure no lumps of fish have escaped the swift turning blade. You have to have a perfectly smooth mix. Mix in the final egg, then remove the sole mix from the machine, put in a dish, and cover with cling film. Leave it and the salmon-lined ramekins in the fridge overnight, or for up to 24 hours.

The next day, pre-heat the oven to gas mark 6, 400°F (200°C).

When you take the sole out, it will be quite gelatinous, and in a lump like a choux pastry dough gone cold before the eggs are added! Return to your processor and then dribble in the double cream very, very slowly, with long gaps in between additions. The mixture will be ice-cream-like, and should either be piped or spooned into the 6 ramekins. Push the asparagus tips gently into the middle. You *can* cover them again with cling film and leave in the fridge for 2–3 hours before cooking, but they're better if all this above is done immediately prior to cooking.

Place in a bain-marie with some hot water, and then into the pre-heated oven, and cook for 20–30 minutes. Remove from the oven and leave them for 2–3 minutes (possibly while you finish off the hollandaise) in a *draught-free* place, allowing them to settle just a little. They are then quite easy to turn out on to one hand and then on to your warm serving plate. Surround with the warm hollandaise and garnish with Keta and fresh dill.

VARIATIONS

Having mastered this procedure you can ring the changes by using chicken breast (particularly delicious if marinated for 2–3 days in natural yoghurt and then wiped fairly dry before starting the recipe off), fillets of pork or bits of veal in place of fish. Bacon could be wrapped round the sides of these ramekins. If you decide to use chicken breasts, very finely chopped root vegetables may be folded into the final mixture before being spooned into the ramekins; in this case these could be lined with blanched lettuce or spinach leaves (stalks removed, naturally).

Even further experimenting can be done. Place only half the fish mixture in the ramekin, top with a fresh scallop, then top off with more of the fish mixture. With a chicken mix, a chicken or duck liver may be put in the middle. The permutations are endless and if you come up with something very original and unique, I would be happy to hear about it!

CHESTNUT-STUFFED FILLET STEAK WRAPPED IN BACON

———·· ———

Fillet steak (tenderloin in the States) is always nice and tender but I think it has little flavour, and I never order it when dining out. It is, in fact, the undercut from the sirloin, and at Miller Howe, after the whole sirloins have been hung on the bone for at least 3 weeks, the full fillet is removed and the small tail end (filet mignon) removed in turn. (This latter is smeared with olive oil, lightly seasoned, then wrapped in cling film and foil and frozen. When enough have accumulated, I cut them into strips for the recipe on p. 154, an easy task, as a good kitchen knife simply glides through the flesh.)

The steaks for this dish are cut from the fatter part of the fillet. It will be very popular with guests – also with *you*, as it can be prepared way ahead of time. When cooking, too, it only needs turning once. No hassle!

· *per person* ·

1 fillet steak, $1\frac{1}{2}$ in (4 cm) thick and weighing about 6 oz
(175 g)
2 fresh chestnuts, peeled
1 rasher good smoked bacon
1 × 3 in (7.5 cm) croûton (p. 127)

for the garnish
1 twirl garlic butter or 2 steamed garlic cloves (see below)

Remove any sign of gristle from each steak, and then make an incision on one side, just over half-way into the steak itself, forming a cavity into which you can stuff the whole fresh chestnuts. Secure the end opening with a wooden toothpick. Trim the smoked bacon so that it will encircle the outer edge of the steak, overlapping slightly, and secure in position with 2 wooden cocktail sticks. All this preparation may be done the day before and then each steak wrapped in cling film and unwrapped just prior to cooking.

When you wish to cook, pre-heat the oven to gas mark 8, 450°F (230°C). For medium cooking – the way *I* like them – the steaks need 6 minutes on each side, that's all. Served on the croûtons, and garnished with the steamed garlic or a large piped twirl of garlic butter, they make a meal fit for a king.

GARLIC BUTTER

——— · • · ———

· *makes $\frac{1}{2}$ lb (225 g)* ·

8 oz (225 g) soft salted butter
3 garlic cloves

Beat the very soft salted butter in a mixing bowl, and then beat in the peeled and crushed garlic cloves.

STEAMED GARLIC

——— · • · ———

Steaming garlic takes away the strong flavour and makes it palatable to most folk. Place a colander on top of a saucepan of simmering water. Get a whole bulb of garlic and patiently skin each clove – or use only as many cloves as you need – and put in the colander. Cover and steam for 5–10 minutes. Served with steaks, lamb or meaty fish, they are quite delicious.

PAN-FRIED FILLET STEAK STRIPS WITH WATERCHESTNUTS AND SOY SAUCE

—— · • · ——

If you want to serve this for eight, simply double the ingredients, but you must cook the strips off in *two* frying-pans at the same time. Use the filets mignons mentioned in the recipe on p. 152.

· *serves 4* ·

12 oz (350 g) fillet steak tail ends
8 tablespoons white wine
4 tablespoons olive oil
4 oz (100 g) onions, peeled and very finely chopped
2 fat garlic cloves, peeled and crushed with salt
8 canned waterchestnuts, drained and roughly chopped
2 tablespoons soy sauce

for the garnish
double cream
chopped parsley

Divide the fillet ends into 4 × 3 oz (75 g) pieces, and then cut each into 10–12 thin strips. Marinate these for about 4 hours in the wine, and then drain (keeping the wine) and dry on kitchen paper.

Heat the olive oil to smoking point, then turn down the heat, and add the chopped onion and crushed garlic. Stir until cooked through, then strain through a metal sieve, retaining what little oil comes out. Return this to the frying-pan, turn up the heat again, and add the steak strips. Sizzle away to seal the meat all over, then pour on the marinade wine and cook over vicious heat until the wine evaporates.

Throw in the chopped waterchestnuts, and the onion and garlic mixture, then add the soy sauce. Stir this through, and serve immediately with mashed potato or cooked rice. A smear of warmed dribbling cream gives this a rich finish and a generous sprinkling of chopped parsley as it is being served adds a little colour.

Boned Stuffed Leg of Lamb

—— · • · ——

The stuffing for this roast is delicious, rather Greek in influence.

· serves 6–8 ·

1 boned leg of lamb, weighing approx. 4½ lb (2 kg) after boning
8 garlic cloves, peeled
4 oz (100 g) soft butter
salt and freshly ground black pepper

for the stuffing
4 oz (100 g) savoury breadcrumbs (p. 147)
4 oz (100 g) onions, peeled and finely chopped
18 black olives, with stones
8 oz (225 g) Feta cheese, roughly chopped
6 firm tomatoes, skinned, seeded and cut into wedges
6 tablespoons finely chopped fresh herbs
1 generous teaspoon ground cinnamon
3 eggs, beaten

Pre-heat the oven to gas mark 8, 450°F (230°C).

Trim the boned leg of any excess fat or gristle and lay flat on the work-top, bone hole upwards.

Mix all the stuffing ingredients together, binding them with the beaten eggs. Place on top of the boned meat, and roll up into as even a shape as possible, tying with circles of strong kitchen twine. Make 8 incisions into the meat with a small, sharp pointed knife, and into these incisions, push the garlic cloves. Smear all over with the soft butter and season with salt and pepper. Wrap up in a large piece of foil, dull side inwards.

Place in the oven in a baking tin and roast for 1 hour in the foil. Remove the foil and continue roasting for a further hour for well-done lamb.

VEGETABLE ACCOMPANIMENTS

One of the main difficulties when entertaining is to calmly get the act together so that there is no strain for hosts or guests alike. When it comes to vegetables, they are often just barely cooked or done to high heaven, resulting in diners having to put on a brave face and go crunch, crunch, or resorting to a dessertspoon to scoop up the slush! And I sympathise with hosts/hostesses who have other jobs to attend to as well as the basic cooking – drinks to pour, starters to see to, kids to calm etc.

I am an avid lover of fresh vegetables, and also adore the company of my guests when entertaining at home on the Sunday evenings I have off from working in the hotel. So, all the following recipes have certainly helped me a great deal when having people in for a meal, as everything can be basically prepared well in advance, in the morning, needing only a little last-minute cooking!

A PLATTER OF PARTY VEGETABLES

· *serves 4* ·

4 oz (100 g) each of carrots and turnips, peeled and cut into
strips the size of your little finger
4 small courgettes, topped, tailed and scored
4 oz (100 g) French beans, topped and tailed
salt and freshly ground black pepper
2 oz (50 g) butter

Have ready a metal sieve that will drop inside a pan of boiling seasoned water and, close by, a bowl of ice-cold water into which the sieve will also fit. Place the four lots of vegetables, one lot at a time, in the sieve and into the pan of boiling salted water. As soon as it comes back to the boil, be most meticulous about timing, for each vegetable is to cook for *2 minutes only*. Take the sieve out of the boiling water and immediately submerge in the bowl of ice-cold water to arrest the cooking process.

You need now a suitable serving dish which you are eventually going to use at the party and a round 1 in (2.5 cm) deep Pyrex pie plate is fine. You want something that will look good on the night and that will adequately hold the four cooked vegetables. These are attractively arranged – I usually put the two green vegetables opposite each other and the carrots and turnips either side.

In a small saucepan, gently melt the butter and pour over the arranged vegetables. Season well with salt and freshly ground black pepper. Cover completely with foil and when stone cold put in the fridge.

On the party evening, reheat the dish in an oven pre-heated to gas mark 5, 375°F (190°C) for 25 minutes to really warm through and finish off the cooking.

BRUSSELS SPROUTS WITH BACON

· *serves 4* ·

20 sprouts, trimmed and outer leaves removed
2 oz (50 g) smoked bacon, rinded and finely diced
1 garlic clove, peeled (optional)
1 tablespoon cooking oil
freshly ground black pepper

Make a very neat criss-cross incision into the base of each sprout, then put into a pan of boiling, unseasoned water. Allow to come back to the boil, and simmer gently for *3 minutes only*. Pour into a sieve and place the sprouts under a slow running tap to cool down. Leave in the fridge or a cool place.

Cook the smoked bacon dice in a frying pan large enough to eventually hold the sprouts. Cook to your own personal taste – slightly underdone or crisp – and then remove from the heat. (I like to use a little garlic with the sprouts: mash the peeled clove to a paste with a knife, and cook with the diced bacon at this stage.)

When you wish to serve the sprouts at a party, simply add the cooking oil to the cooked bacon in the frying pan and bring up to smoking point. Toss in the partly cooked sprouts, season with some pepper, and fry for 2–3 minutes.

DICED LEEKS COOKED IN WHITE WINE WITH TOASTED ALMONDS

· serves 4 ·

4 medium leeks, topped and tailed
1 oz (25 g) soft butter
4 tablespoons white wine

for the garnish
4 teaspoons toasted flaked almonds

Slice the leeks very finely *crosswise, not* lengthwise. Put into a sieve and wash thoroughly underneath a running tap, watching keenly to ensure there is no muck left in. Leave to drain and then dry off on kitchen paper. Keep cool.

When you wish to cook them (and they take such a short time), heat the butter gently in a small pan, add the wine and bring up to the boil. Throw in the dried, cleaned leeks and cook over a high heat for 3–4 minutes, stirring occasionally. Using a slotted spoon transfer to the serving plates and then garnish with the flaked toasted almonds.

RICH DICED POTATOES

· serves 4 ·

2 oz (50 g) butter
4 oz (100 g) onions, peeled and finely diced
12 oz (350 g) potatoes, peeled and cubed
salt and freshly ground black pepper
10 fl oz (300 ml) milk

Melt the butter in a small saucepan and fry the diced onion until nice and golden. Remove and drain on kitchen paper. Put the potatoes in the pan with the oniony butter, season with salt and pepper, and cook until brown. Add the drained onions and the milk. At this stage the pan may be covered and left to one side in a cool place until you need the dish.

When you're ready to cook, simply bring the potatoes back to the boil, and gently simmer for 10 minutes.

BLENDER HOLLANDAISE

———— ·•· ————

A normal liquidiser or blender will take 8 oz (225 g) butter when making hollandaise, but a food processor can take up to 1 lb (450 g) and slightly more. Vary the proportions accordingly. Hollandaise is better made at the last minute as it can then be served nice and hot, but if made in a food processor 10 minutes before it's needed, you can leave it on at the lowest speed, and the sauce will come to no harm – it only gets slightly cooler. What *is* essential, though, is a jug with an excellent pouring lip which will enable the hot lemon juice and then the bubbling butter to slowly trickle on to the egg yolk mixture.

To vary your hollandaise, you could use different vinegars. Tarragon vinegar, for instance, will give you the right flavour for the salmon on page 43, but now that there are various different vinegars on the market, experiment with garlic, mint and herb etc for other dishes. You can also *add* ingredients, as with blender mayonnaise (p. 57), to vary the basic hollandaise: tomato purée, more citrus juice, herbs, avocado, horseradish and mustard.

· *serves 6* ·

1 tablespoon chosen vinegar (*not* malt!)
3 tablespoons fresh lemon juice
8 oz (225 g) butter
4 egg yolks
1 teaspoon caster sugar
a pinch of salt

Put the vinegar and lemon juice into a small pan and heat to bubbling. Melt the butter in another pan.

Put the egg yolks, sugar and salt into the blender and mix for a while. Put on top speed and start to trickle in the boiling vinegar and lemon juice from that good pouring jug. When this has been absorbed, put the hot melted butter in the jug and trickle this in as well. When this is absorbed, your hollandaise is ready. Serve hot.

FRUIT TERRINE SLICE

——— · • · ———

A rich, but simple to prepare, dish which looks very pretty on the plate. The fruit used can be varied according to the season.

· serves 12 ·

4 oz (100 g) soft unsalted butter
3 oz (75 g) caster sugar
2 tablespoons orange curaçao, Van der Hum or other
suitable liqueur
10 fl oz (300 ml) double cream, beaten to a ribbon
3 oz (75 g) ground hazelnuts

fruit (vary with season)
3 bananas, peeled and thinly sliced
4 oranges, peeled and segmented (p. 10)
8 oz (225 g) strawberries, thinly sliced
3 kiwi fruit, peeled and thinly sliced
$\frac{1}{2}$ Ogen melon, peeled and thinly sliced
2 oz (50 g) red or black currants (if available)

apricot purée
1 × 1 lb (450 g) can apricots, drained
a touch of brandy
a touch of icing sugar

Lightly grease or oil a normal terrine mould – 14 × 3 × 3 in (35 × 7.5 × 7.5 cm) – and then carefully line the base and sides with cling film.

Cream the butter and sugar together until fluffy and white, then little by little add the chosen liqueur. Fold in the beaten cream along with the ground hazelnuts. This is the basic 'binding mix'.

Pipe a thin layer of the cream mixture on to the base of the lined terrine, and press down the thinly sliced bananas. Follow this up to the top, alternating the vari-coloured fruits with the cream. Finish with a cream layer. Leave for 6–8 hours to chill.

Meanwhile make the apricot purée. Simply work the dried drained apricots, brandy and sugar to a purée in the blender. Taste and add more brandy or sugar if necessary.

Turn the terrine out on to a serving plate carefully, using the edges of the cling film to help it out. It is easily sliced if you use a serrated carving knife dipped into hot water between each slice. Serve each slice on top of a spoonful or so of apricot purée, spread out across the plate.

Fruit Purées

———·———

Served for breakfast with thick natural yoghurt and some toasted nuts, these are delicious and healthy; but they could be used as a garnish for a savoury main course – pineapple purée underneath a portion of the roast chicken on p. 49 is wonderful. They could of course be served as a dinner party pudding as well: triple stacked in knickerbocker type glasses as on p. 143, or simply portioned out in three blobs around a lipped dish with a portion of sorbet in the middle.

· *makes 1 pint (600 ml) of each purée* ·

mango
3 average sized medium mangoes

pineapple
1 medium pineapple

apple
6 Granny Smith apples
2 oz (50 g) butter
juice and finely grated rind of 2 limes
2 tablespoons soft brown sugar

The mango and pineapple purées are simplicity itself. Liquidise the flesh of each to a purée, and pass through a sieve into bowls. The apples should be chopped then cooked until soft in the butter with the lime rind and juice and sugar. When soft, liquidise and pass through a sieve.

Chocolate Shortbread Tartlets with Chocolate Orange Cream

———— · • · ————

Quite apart from specially making these for entertaining or a special meal, they are handy to have stored away in an airtight tin (they store well for a couple of weeks). They make a few strawberries with whipped cream go much further should unheralded guests descend; or the mousse on p. 164 can be popped into them providing an alternative filling to that given below, and could be a good packed lunch addition or a supper snack. It's best to use individual fluted tins, but they can be made in the 9 or 12 bun-tin sets. Seek out individual cake cases made from good greaseproof paper and your task will be easier.

Many years ago we had to do the pudding for over 600 people at the old Quaglino's for the International Convention of the Wine and Food Society and these tartlets were all taken down from the Lakes to London on the train, stored in airtight containers. Even with the handling of British Rail porters, I think there were only three damaged when we set them out to fill with the chocolate orange cream. On that occasion, if my memory is correct, a teaspoon of butterscotch sauce (p. 77) was placed on the base as well!

The chocolate orange cream filling makes a good pudding on its own.

· *makes 12 individual 3 in (7.5 cm) tartlets* ·

4 oz (100 g) plain flour
2 oz (50 g) Farola or semolina
2 oz (50 g) caster sugar
4 oz (100 g) soft butter

for the chocolate lining
3 oz (75 g) good chocolate, broken into pieces
1 tablespoon rum

chocolate orange cream
8 oz (225 g) good chocolate, broken into pieces
juice and finely grated rind of 1 orange
3 tablespoons orange curaçao
2 egg yolks
15 fl oz (450 ml) double cream
3 oz (75 g) caster sugar, sieved

Place all the shortbread ingredients into your mixer and combine slowly to form a dough. Divide into 12 even-sized balls.

Place a cake case inside each tin or 'bun hole' and place a ball of the dough inside this. Then, using your thumb, quite roughly, ease this all over the base and up the sides to the top. If you are using individual tins you will find the task simpler as any surplus dough can easily be disposed of! Rest in the fridge for at least an hour, and meanwhile pre-heat the oven to gas mark 2, 300°F (150°C).

Put a further paper cake base *inside* the shortbread lining, and fill with either rice, dried peas or dry macaroni. Bake the tartlets in the pre-heated oven for 45–60 minutes, until firm to the touch. As they are cooling, remove carefully from the containers.

To make the chocolate lining – this also strengthens the shortbread bases – put the chocolate and rum in a small bowl over a pan of simmering water and melt together. Pour a generous teaspoon of this on to the base of each tartlet. Tip on its side so that the chocolate runs up to the top edge all round. As this cools, so it will stiffen and make the edges quite secure.

To make the chocolate orange cream, put the chocolate, orange juice and rind, and orange curaçao in a bowl over simmering water and melt together. When cool, beat in the egg yolks. In a separate bowl, beat the double cream to a peak with the sugar. Combine both mixtures, folding carefully together, and then pipe into the prepared shortbread tartlets. Try to do this as near as possible to the time you wish to serve with this cream, although you'll have to do it ahead if you're using the mousse mixture on p. 164.

Orange Mousse

———··———

A mousse at the end of a dinner party is light and refreshing, and as it can be made the night before, it's a handy recipe to have for entertaining. A nice alternative way of serving it is to spoon it into the shortbread tartlets on p. 162.

· *fills 10–12 × 3 in (7.5 cm) ramekins or 24 tartlets* ·

$\frac{1}{2}$ oz (15 g) powdered gelatine
3 tablespoons orange curaçao plus 2 tablespoons water
3 eggs, plus 2 egg yolks
2 oz (50 g) caster sugar, sieved
10 fl oz (300 ml) double cream
1 × 6$\frac{3}{4}$ fl oz (178 ml) can frozen concentrated orange juice,
defrosted
finely grated rind of 2 oranges

Put the gelatine in a small saucepan and add the orange curaçao and water all in one go. Leave to one side (p. 79).

Warm your mixer bowl and beaters, and put the eggs and egg yolks into the bowl. Beat away on the highest speed for about 8 minutes, then start to add the sugar little by little. Please don't do this too quickly, or the volume of the eggs will diminish. Add the sugar tablespoon by tablespoon at the most.

In a separate bowl, beat up the double cream until it is roughly of the same texture as the eggs – soft peak – then fold in the orange juice and the finely grated orange rind.

Turn the egg mixture out of the mixer bowl into a large plastic bowl, and fold in the flavoured whipped cream lightly.

Reconstitute the gelatine by warming *gently* until the liquid is clear (p. 79), and then add to the mixture through a warmed metal sieve. Fold it in with sharp determined moves in that figure-of-eight action. Pour the mixture into a jug with a good pouring lip and then into the individual ramekins (or tartlet bases). If you don't have ramekins, wine or cocktail glasses will do. Put in the fridge, covered, to set, which will take about 8 hours. *Never* freeze.

You can vary this recipe slightly by adding 3 level tablespoons chopped mint to the cream. Put fresh orange segments (p. 10) on the base of the ramekins before filling up with the finished mousse mixture.

PEARS POACHED IN CIDER

· serves 6 ·

6 firm pears, about 2 lb (900 g) in weight, peeled and cored
(leave the stalks on as they look pretty)
$1\frac{1}{4}$ pints (750 ml) cider of choice

to serve
see method

Cut a thin slice off the fat bottom of each pear, so that it will stand upright. Place the pears, stalks up, in a saucepan and then cover with the cider. Simmer for 20 minutes and they are ready to eat hot, or they can be left to go cold.

To serve hot, you could reduce the cider to a tacky jelly along with the juice and finely grated rind of 1 orange or a couple of tablespoons of redcurrant jelly. Pour this over and around the pears.

To serve cold, you could arrange each pear on a base of thick natural yoghurt and scatter with fresh raspberries or wild Alpine strawberries. Garnish with sprigs of fresh garden mint.

Deep-fried Dates Stuffed with Hazelnut and Orange

———— · • · ————

· *serves 6–8* ·

24 orange segments (p. 10)
2 oz (50 g) ground hazelnuts
24 fresh dates, peeled and stoned
good vegetable oil for deep-frying

batter
4 oz (100 g) strong plain flour, sieved
a pinch of salt
2 eggs, separated
5 fl oz (150 ml) milk
2 tablespoons olive oil

to serve
ground cinnamon or nutmeg, icing sugar, whipped cream

Make the batter first – *at least* 4 hours ahead of frying. Put the flour into a bowl with the salt. Beat the egg yolks with the milk and olive oil, and slowly beat this into the flour using an electric hand mixer. Leave to rest.

Meanwhile, toss the orange segments in the ground hazelnuts. Stuff each fresh date with a coated orange segment.

Just prior to deep-frying – at about 350°F (180°C) – beat the 2 egg whites quite stiff and fold into the rested batter. Coat the dates well, then deep-fry in the hot oil for 2–3 minutes until brown. Remove to a double thickness of kitchen paper, and serve dusted with ground cinnamon or nutmeg mixed with icing sugar along with dollops of sweetened cream.

INDEX

————··————

Italic page numbers indicate a colour illustration.

167